Alma. M

23. The Town

Gt Stoughton

POPULAR
ANTIQUES
and their
VALUES
1800~1875

Compiled and Edited by
TONY CURTIS

While every care has been taken in the compiling of information contained in this volume the publishers cannot accept any liability for loss, financial or otherwise, incurred by reliance placed on the information herein.

All prices quoted in this book are obtained from a variety of auctions in various countries and are converted to dollars at the rate of exchange prevalent at the time of sale.

ISBN 0-86248-026-4

Copyright © Lyle Publications MCMLXXXIII
Published by Lyle Publications, Glenmayne, Galashiels, Selkirkshire, Scotland.

Printed and bound by Hazell Watson & Viney Ltd, Aylesbury, Bucks

INTRODUCTION

ond its purely aesthetic appeal, an cle of a bygone age frequently has great advantage over that which is duced at the present time: it gener- appreciates in value as each year ses and few people in this day and would disagree with the proposition t a beautiful piece whose investment ential may be as high as that of pro- ty is an asset indeed.

purpose of this publication is to ke it easy for those either buying, ng, or merely interested in the value the pieces in their own home, to tify and have a knowledge of the e an Antique Dealer is likely to pay a piece in average condition.

items chosen are, on the whole, re- sentative of the middle section of the ket with the addition of a few rare es, which, although not to be found every corner shop, command such rrisingly high prices as to make their usion of benefit to the reader.

current value of an Antique varies rmously in different areas. What is ionable in one county may be lly disregarded in another, which unts for the amount of trading be-

tween dealers who come from different parts of the country. This will also happen when one dealer is more knowledgeable than another or a specialist in a particular field. One dealer may find it more profitable to turn his stock over frequently in order to keep his money 'working' for him and will therefore buy and sell while showing a very modest profit. Another may treat his stock as an investment and can afford to wait for a higher price.

When making any calculations it is wise to remember that the dealer may have to spend as much having the piece put in a saleable condition as he has originally paid for that same item. One must also allow for his profit margin. At all times the cost of restoration must be taken into account, for even the most rare piece, if damaged is imperfect, and therefore of lesser value than the perfect example.

It will, however, give a fair idea of the value which I hope will be of assistance to those who, while having an appreciation of the look and feel of antiques, lack the confidence to plunge in at the deep end.

TONY CURTIS

CONTENTS

BAROMETERS

Admiral Fitzroy barometer in an oak case. $225 £100

Mid 19th century barometer in cast iron case, 24½in. high. $381 £165

Attractive wheel barometer in rosewood, circa 1840, 40½in. high. $450 £200

Early Victorian wheel or banjo barometer, circa 1850, 40in. high. $553 £245

Wheel barometer in rosewood case, circa 1830, 43in. high. $621 £275

Mahogany eight inch wheel barometer, circa 1820, 3ft.2½in. long. $675 £300

19th century stick barometer. $790 £350

Early 19th century barometer. $1,070 £475

Early 19th century mahogany stick barometer, signed T. Dunn, Edinburgh, 3ft.1in. high. $1,125 £500

Mother-of-pearl inlaid rosewood barometer, circa 1850, 44¾in. high. $1,125 £500

Rosewood wheel barometer with silvered dial, by J. Somalvico & Son, circa 1820, 38in. high. $1,295 £575

Mid 19th century mahogany stick barometer, by B. Martin, London, 90cm. high. $2,815 £580

Fine quality large 19th century mahogany carved banjo barometer with clock. $1,350 £600

Inlaid mahogany stick barometer, by Negrety, 1850, 44in. long. $1,630 £725

19th century mahogany marine barometer, by J. Morton & Co., Glasgow, 36in. high. $1,745 £775

th century French bronze ust of Raphael, signed A. rtier. $170 £75

A bronze plaque of Napoleon, circa 1850, 10in. diam.
$170 £75

Regency period ormolu reel stand with the original reels. $170 £75

19th century bronze devil mask of Lucifer with a rasping tongue, 9in. high.
$225 £100

ne of a pair of early 19th ntury bronze urns, 9in. gh. $300 £135

Mid 19th century bronze incense burner and cover, 51cm. high. $460 £200

Bronze figure of a grazing ewe, by Rosa Bonheur, circa 1860, 6in. wide.
$520 £230

Bronze model of a nef, mid 19th century, 18¼in. high.
$520 £230

farmer on horseback, arrowing, signed 'E. rouot', on a rouge arble base, 17in. wide.
$620 £275

Bronze figure, by Eugene Laurent, 14¼in. high, circa 1870. $640 £285

19th century Italian bronze of a kneeling boy, by Girba Franti. $675 £300

Bronze figure of a hunter, 42cm. high, restraining a dog. $725 £320

th century study of a te player in bronze, cm. high. $745 £330

Mid 19th century bronze group, by Charles Cumberworth, 13½in. high.
$845 £375

19th century classical bronze figure group, 41cm. high.
$945 £420

19th century French bronze of a swordsman.
$1,015 £450

One of a pair of gilt bronze candelabra, 27in. high, 1870's. $1,000 £450

19th century French bronze group, signed L. Longpied, 19in. high. $1,080 £480

Pair of large mid 19th century bronze firedogs.
$1,125 £500

Large 19th century bronze study, signed Myrver, 60cm. high. $1,125 £50

Japanese bronze eagle on tree trunk with snake at base. $1,350 £600

19th century Italian bronze figure of Cupid, 3ft.1in. high. $1,350 £600

One of a pair of 19th century bronze ewer ornaments. $1,530 £680

19th century bronze figure of an old man, 9in. long.
$1,540 £685

A French bronze group of two pointers with a dead hare, signed P. J. Mene, dated 1872, 8in. long. $1,575 £700

19th century Japanese bronze figure of a Samurai warrior, 10in. high.
$2,025 £900

One of a pair of Venetian 'Renaissance' bronze torcheres, circa 1870, 48in. high.
$2,030 £920

Pair of 19th century bronze figures of musicians 20in. high. $2,140 £95

19th century bronze figure of Ulysses, 35in. high.
$2,700 £1,200,

Mid 19th century bronze group of Una and the Lion, signed G. Geefs, 43.2cm. high.
$2,925 £1,300

A bronze racehorse and jockey, signed I. Bonheur, circa 1860, 18½in. long.
$3,150 £1,400

19th century bronze model of a seated tiger 24½in. high.
$5,175 £2,30

Toleware circular spice cabinet, circa 1835, 6¼in. diam. $63 £28

Victorian Chinese ivory cricket box, circa 1840, 3½in. wide. $80 £35

Regency rosewood tea caddy, with mother-of-pearl inlaid lid, 35cm. wide. $87 £38

Victorian rosewood stationery box with brass fittings. $110 £48

Regency rosewood tea caddy with bombe front, 37cm. wide. $115 £50

Carved oak letter box, circa 1860. $120 £55

Circular pollard wood snuff box, circa 1820, 8.5cm. diam. $145 £65

Sheraton period tea caddy, circa 1800, 7in. wide, in mahogany with ebony stringing. $146 £65

Victorian satinwood and crossbanded square shaped tea caddy, 13.5cm. wide. $180 £80

19th century Japanese lacquer cigar case, 5in. wide. $192 £85

Victorian coromandelwood box, by Baxter, London, 1856, 8½in. wide.$190 £85

Box made from a coco-de-mer and carved to resemble a peacock. $205 £95

9th century painted satinwood Sheraton design velvet lined box. $250 £110

Mid 19th century coromandelwood tea caddy, 38cm. wide.$270 £120

Mid 19th century tortoise-shell and silvered metal mounted box. $270 £120

Victorian papier mache sewing box. $295 £145

11

Regency tea caddy, inlaid with brass and mother-of-pearl floral design. $370 £165

Early 19th century Chinese export black and gold lacquer toilet mirror base, 19½in. wide. $450 £200

Early 19th century tortoiseshell tea caddy, inlaid with mother-of-pearl. $450 £200

19th century lacquer Suzuribako, 9¼in. wide. $565 £250

19th century lacquered box and cover, Japanese, 22cm. wide. $565 £250

19th century Persian papier mache scribe's pen box, 12in. long. $600 £265

Mid 19th century red boulle encrier, lid opening to reveal letter compartments. $700 £310

Tortoiseshell and mother-of-pearl inlaid tea caddy. $730 £325

 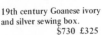   

19th century Goanese ivory and silver sewing box. $730 £325

Victorian burr-walnut writing slope with brass mounts, 1ft.2in. wide, circa 1880. $1,039 £460

Early 19th century French musical necessaire, 7.5cm. wide. $1,125 £500

One of a fine pair of mahogany knife boxes with inlaid conch shells $1,125 £500

Pair of late Victorian urn-shaped decanter boxes, 31in. high. $1,835 £850

Coachbuilder's tool chest and contents, tools bearing the stamp of J. Hartley, circa 1839. $3,164 £1,400

Finely carved Oriental needlework box, fitted with compartments and ivory tools. $3,580 £1,550

Good Alphonse Giroux miniature casket, circa 1850, 16in. wide. $3,224 £1,550

Olivewood Scandinavian carved jug, with carved pattern, 4¼in. high, circa 1860. $63 £28

Good Toleware polished chamberstick, circa 1840, 2½in. high, by H. F. & Co. $63 £28

Beechwood butter marker, circa 1840, 4½in. diam. $79 £35

Early 19th century pine-wood bowl, possibly American, 15in. diam. $146 £65

Lignum Vitae apothecary's mortar, 5¼in. high, circa 1800. $145 £65

Shield-shaped family horse coach panel, circa 1840, 17½in. wide. $192 £85

One of a pair of 19th century carved wood models of stags, 8in. high. $198 £88

19th century Oriental gong with carved hardwood stand. $225 £100

Interesting carved wood Chinese figure of a seated god, 19in. high. $226 £105

Italian carved wood Jester's head, circa 1860. $292 £130

19th century carved wood 'Bateka'. $315 £146

Fruitwood watch stand, 230mm. high. $415 £185

Mid 19th century Scandinavian painted pine butter tub and cover. $505 £225

Mid 19th century giltwood door frame, 64in. wide. $530 £235

19th century oak figure of Henry VIII. $565 £250

19th century human face mask of the Senufo tribe, 13½in. high. $640 £285

13

19th century Dutch cart front decorated in polychrome.
$675 £300

Early 19th century Dutch carved oak carriage foot-warmer with brass handle, 9¼in. wide. $780 £340

Early 19th century Chinese gold lacquer figure on an ebonised and gilt base, 23in. high.
$1,125 £500

Austrian carved walnut umbrella stand, 81in. high, 1870's.
$1,622 £780

Fine mid 19th century Italian ship's figurehead from The Benvolio.$2,147 £950

19th century Swiss bear furniture.$2,250 £1,000

Early 19th century toabacconist's sign of a Highlander.
$2,250 £1,000

CHANDELIERS

Regency twelve-light brass chandelier with glass drops.
$675 £300

Regency gilt brass Kolza oil lantern, 2ft.1in. diam., circa 1820. $675 £300

19th century French rococo style brass chandelier, 21in. wide. $900 £400

19th century crystal chandelier with ten scrolled ormolu arms, 3ft.6in. high.
$1,235 £550

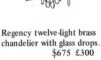

Restoration hanging Kolza lamp, circa 1820, 2ft.6in. diam. $1,350 £600

Early 19th century bronze chandelier of eighteen lamps, 2ft.3½in. diam.
$1,600 £715

A crisply cast nine-light ormolu chandelier, Paris, 1850. $2,250 £1,000

George III cut glass eight-light chandelier, 43in. high.
$5,065 £2,250

Child's plate with the heading 'Pilgrim's Progress', circa 1845, 7¼in. diam. $55 £25

Scottish pottery Glasgow cup, saucer and plate. $70 £30

William Brownfield salt-glaze jug, 1868, decorated with vine leaves. $70 £30

Mid 19th century Jackfield pottery cow creamer jug, circa 1840, 5¼in. high. $80 £35

Blue and white lavatory pan, 'Niagara'. $170 £75

Amusing Cumnock pottery hen salt crock, 1872, 29.5cm. high. $215 £95

Pearlware tea caddy of canted rectangular form, 13cm. high, circa 1860. $225 £100

Dawson & Co. creamware cylindrical tankard, 4¾in. high. $225 £100

Set of Victorian glazed tiles depicting a maltster, now made into a coffee table top. $295 £130

Part of an early 19th century earthenware dessert service, nineteen pieces. $485 £215

Newcastle pearlware cow group, circa 1800, 12.5cm. wide. $540 £240

Part of a Hicks, Meigh & Johnson ironstone service, circa 1822-35. $1,000 £445

CANTON

Early 19th century Canton porcelain vase with flared neck, 24in. high. $270 £120

Part of a mid 19th century coffee set of six pieces. $480 £210

19th century Canton enamel porcelain bowl, decorated overall with figures and flowers, 18¾in. diam. $945 £420

A large early 19th century Canton enamel jardiniere, decorated with scenic views. $970 £430

A 19th century Chinese porcelain jardiniere, 7in. diam. $90 £40

Oviform blue and white Chinese vase with lid, circa 1859, 1ft.2½in. high. $135 £60

One of ten Chinese 19th century wine tasting cups, 2½in. diam. $170 £75

A Chinese unglazed pottery standing figure in gathered robes wearing a dignitary's crown. $170 £75

A blue and white Chinese porcelain lidded jug decorated with figures. $190 £85

19th century Chinese bottle-shaped vase with dragon decorations. $225 £100

Early 19th century Chinese censer with wood and jade lid. $225 £100

Early 19th century Chinese sang de boeuf vase in ovoid form. $225 £100

Chinese blue and white vase, decorated with domestic scenes, 19in. high. $315 £140

19th century Chinese blue and white bulbous vase and cover on stand. $450 £200

Early 19th century Chinese blue and white moonflask, decorated with a domestic scene, 46cm. high. $500 £230

Early 19th century Chinese porcelain Buddha. $730 £325

One of a pair of Chinese blue and white jardinieres, 1830. $745 £330

Early 19th century blue and white bidet of pear-shape, 61.5cm. long. $900 £400

18th/19th century blanc-de-chine group of a lady and a scholar, 7¼in. wide. $1,150 £500

One of a pair of 19th century Chinese famille jaune barrel garden seats. $1,295 £575

albrookdale pot pourri
e, cover and stand, 6¾in.
h. $325 £145

Coalbrookdale two-
handled cabinet cup, cover
and stand, 5½in. tall.
          $395 £175

One of a pair of Coalbrookdale vases, 1820's, 8in.
high. $475 £220

Coalbrookdale flower-encrus-
ted vase surmounted by a
putto. $1,350 £600

ALPORT

Porcelain dessert dish by
Coalport, circa 1835.
          $150 £65

Coalport teapot, circa
1840-45, with elaborate
rococo twirls at handle
base, lid and spout.
          $170 £75

Coalport figure of the Duke
of Wellington, circa 1852,
10¼in. high. $430 £190

One of a pair of wine coolers and covers, probably
Coalport, 11½in. tall, early
19th century.$1,395 £620

MMEMORATIVE

ilway mug, circa 1840,
. high. $160 £70

William IV and Queen
Adelaide coronation mug,
circa 1831, 5in. high.
          $420 £185

Rare commemorative jug,
5½in. high, probably 1832.
          $700 £310

Earthenware coronation
mug of Queen Victoria.
          $1,690 £750

PELAND

ne of a pair of
opeland & Garrett
apan pattern New
tone plates, 21.5cm.
iam. $70 £30

Copeland Parian fig-
ure of Sir Walter
Scott, circa 1860,
11¾in. high.
          $675 £300

Part of a Copeland Spode
seventeen-piece dessert
service. $675 £300

Copeland & Garrett
figure of Narcissus
by John Gibson,
1846, 31cm. high.
          $790 £350

DAOGUANG

Baluster shaped porcelain vase decorated with famille rose enamels, Daoguang period, 7¼in. $80 £35

Small, Daoguang period, famille rose ruby ground bowl with floral decoration and scenic views in panels. $730 £325

Chinese porcelain orchid vase of the Daoguang period. $790 £350

Daoguang blue and white circular sweetmeat dish and cover, 13½in. diam. $1,530 £680

DAVENPORT

A Davenport Longport dessert plate, circa 1770. $35 £15

Davenport cup and saucer, circa 1870. $45 £20

Part of a Davenport tea and coffee service, circa 1870, sixty-one pieces. $350 £155

Part of a twenty-four piece Davenport dessert service, 1870's. $1,575 £700

DERBY

Derby 'Tithe Pig' group, by Stevenson & Hancock, circa 1865, 22cm. high. $360 £160

Early 19th century Bloor Derby veilleuse in three parts, 22.5cm. high. $425 £190

Early 19th century Derby tureen and cover, 14in. wide. $640 £285

Bloor Derby floral encrusted bough pot and cover. $900 £40...

DRESDEN

19th century Dresden group of a boy standing beside a female who is feeding birds, 6in. high. $340 £150

Mid 19th century Dresden shell vase. $620 £275

19th century Dresden centrepiece decorated with figures. $1,060 £470

Pair of early 19th century Dresden figures of a lady and a gallant. $2,250 £1,00...

18

Mid 19th century famille rose oviform vase, 17in. high. $315 £140

Famille rose globular teapot and shallow domed cover, 7¼in. wide. $360 £160

Mid 19th century well painted famille rose screen with carved hardwood stand, 55cm. high. $520 £240

Mid 19th century famille rose jardiniere, 31.8cm. diam. $870 £400

FAMILLE VERTE

Trumpet-shaped famille verte vase, circa 1870, 46.5cm. high. $345 £160

A famille verte tea caddy decorated with vases and flowers. $675 £300

Large famille verte teapot and cover, 10½in. high. $900 £400

Mid 19th century famille verte jardiniere, 40cm. high. $975 £450

IMARI

Mid 19th century Imari porcelain vase, Japanese. $345 £160

Mid 19th century fluted Imari dish, 46.5cm. diam., with basket of flowers in centre. $475 £220

Imari jardiniere in the form of a tied bag, circa 1870, 30.5cm. diam. $565 £260

Japanese Imari vase, circa 1870, 18½in. high. $695 £310

JAPANESE

...th century Japanese porcelain figure, decorated in ...lychrome enamels, 4in. ...h. $90 £40

A mid 19th century Hododa moonflask, 19.5cm. high. $195 £85

One of a pair of Japanese earthenware plates, 23.8cm. diam., circa 1870. $735 £340

Mid 19th century Tomonobu earthenware koro and cover, 20cm. high. $820 £380

19

LIVERPOOL

Liverpool teapot enamelled in black and gilding, Herculaneum factory, circa 1805. $90 £40

Large pottery jug, perhaps Liverpool, 13½in. high, about 1800. $270 £120

Liverpool blue and white meat dish, 14½in. $540 £240

Liverpool creamware mug, signed J. Sadler, 4¼in. high. $595 £265

LUSTRE

Victorian lustre ware goblet with fern decoration, 6in. high. $35 £15

Rare pink lustre jug, 13cm. high, circa 1800-1810. $180 £80

Early 19th century silver lustre pottery figures of Apollo and Diana, 10½in. high. $450 £200

Early 19th century figure of a lion passant, covered in mottled pink lustre, 12in. long. $2,475 £1,100

MAJOLICA

One of a pair of majolica ewer jugs, 19in. high. $95 £40

Large T. C. Brown-Westhead, Moore & Co. majolica vase, 24in. high, circa 1870. $430 £190

Sicilian majolica bottle, 24cm. high. $605 £270

Mid 19th century large majolica urn, stand and pedestal, 150cm. high. $1,195 £530

MASON'S

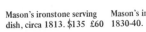

Mason's ironstone serving dish, circa 1813. $135 £60

Mason's inkstand, circa 1830-40. $475 £210

Large hexagonal pot pourri vase, cover and liner, perhaps Mason's, 10½in. high, about 1815-20. $655 £290

Part of a Mason's ironstone dinner and dessert service of sixty-two pieces, 1813-15. $2,365 £1,050

A pair of mid 19th century Meissen cruets, covers and fitted stand, 22.5cm. high. $630 £280

19th century Meissen figure of a lady at her toilet, 5¾in. high. $675 £300

19th century Meissen centrepiece, 8in. high. $785 £350

Good Meissen swan modelled with white plumage, circa 1870, 31cm. high. $1,285 £570

INTON

ine Minton cup and saucer, rca 1870. $80 £35

Pair of Minton parian figures, 14in. high, circa 1858. $430 £190

Good pair of Minton candlesticks, 8½in. high, about 1830. $790 £350

A fine Minton majolica game dish, circa 1870, 13½in. long. $790 £350

ANTGARW

ine Nantgarw plate decoted with five carnations, 4cm. diam., circa 1817. $520 £230

An attractive 'London decorated' Nantgarw plate, 1813-20. $1,350 £600

Rare Nantgarw pedestal dish, 5¾in. high, 1817-20. $1,800 £800

Nantgarw 'London decorated' sucrier and cover, 4in. high, circa 1817-20. $2,250 £1,000

EWHALL

whall jug decorated with igs of flowers, 4½in. high. $115 £50

Rare Newhall water jug with hand-painted Coat of Arms and landscape, circa 1810. $280 £125

Early 19th century Newhall teapot from a thirty-three piece tea and coffee service. $520 £230

Part of a Newhall tea service, twenty-eight pieces, 1795-1805. $675 £300

21

NYMPHENBURG

Nymphenburg model of a parrot, circa 1850-62, 18.7cm. high. $125 £55

One of a pair of Nymphenburg cabinet cups and saucers, 9cm. high, circa 1830-40. $1,125 £500

Porcelain ice-bucket from the Nymphenburg factory, 6½in. high. $1,800 £800

Nymphenburg figure of a parrot, circa 1765, 15.5cm. high, slightly chipped. $4,080 £1,7

ORIENTAL

One of a pair of orange glazed figures of parrots, 7¾in. high. $510 £225

Oriental tureen, stand and cover with floral decoration, 12in. wide. $865 £400

One of a pair of 19th century Kaga baluster vases, 30in. high. $1,350 £600

Good mid 19th century earthenware vase, 12½in. high. $2,815 £1,250

PARIAN

Interesting Bailey Murrells & Co. Parian figure of Palmerston, circa 1865, 17in. high. $215 £95

Well modelled figure, circa 1860, 18¼in. high. $485 £215

Parian bust of Queen Victoria, signed Noble, 2ft. high. $730 £325

Jug showing the famous brass quintet of the Distin father and sons, in Parianware, about 1850, 14in. high. $1,125 £50

PARIS

Paris raspberry ground cache-pot, circa 1870, 18.5cm. high. $295 £130

One of a pair of Feuillet decorated Paris cups and saucers, circa 1840. $430 £190

Attractive Paris part solitaire set, painted with peasants. $540 £240

A good Paris plaque painted by Aumee Lachassaig dated 1834. $1,575 £7

One of a pair of Jacob Petit ...n-shaped porcelain wine ...blers, 12in. high.
$610 £270

One of a pair of Jacob Petit vases, circa 1840, 21.6cm. high. $620 £275

One of a pair of Jacob Petit scent flasks and stoppers, circa 1840, 27cm. high.
$945 £400

One of a pair of Jacob Petit vases, circa 1860.
$960 £425

...OT LIDS

...ood small lid 'Little ...ed Riding Hood'.
$80 £35

English pot lid 'The Net Mender', circa 1860, 4½in. diam. $170 £75

Large pot lid of Queen Victoria on balcony.
$505 £225

Medium sized pot lid of 'Our Pets' with registration mark. $1,070 £475

...OTSCHAPPEL

...e of a pair of late 19th cen-...y Potschappel pot-pourri ...es and covers, 15cm. high.
$240 £100

Potschappel porcelain fruit basket on stand, circa 1860.
$745 £330

A pair of Dresden vases, by Carl Thierne of Pots-chappel, 22½in. high.
$1,295 £575

A fine pair of elaborately decorated Potschappel china jars, 31in. high.
$2,925 £1,300

...RATTWARE

...re Prattware pottery plate ...picting 'The Two Anglers', ...ca 1850, 9½in. diam.
$100 £45

Prattware malachite ground mug 'The Smokers', circa 1860, 4¼in. high. $190 £85

One of a pair of Prattware malachite flasks.
$360 £160

Prattware cockerel standing 10in. tall. $970 £430

23

RIDGWAY

Part of a Ridgway dessert service, circa 1825, nineteen pieces. $250 £110

Large Ridgway Parian group of Venus and Cupid, 1858, 18¾in. high. $420 £185

Part of a twenty-one piece dessert service, circa 1825-35. $735 £325

One of a pair of Ridgway ice pails, covers and liners circa 1815-20. $870 £38

ROCKINGHAM

Small 19th century Rockingham flower encrusted dish with cover. $80 £35

Rockingham scent bottle and stopper with tall neck, circa 1831-42, 16.5cm. high.$425 £190

Rockingham claret ground fluted helmet-shaped basket, circa 1835.$495 £220

A Rockingham style part tea and coffee service of forty-five pieces, circa 1830. $855 £38

SATSUMA

Mid 19th century Satsuma Shi-Shi, 20cm. high. $630 £280

Mid 19th century Satsuma earthenware bowl, 14.5cm. diam. $770 £340

One of a pair of Satsuma vases, 19th century, 7½in. high. $675 £300

Mid 19th century Japanese Satsuma earthenware caddy and cover, 13.5cm. high. $1,035 £46

A 19th century Satsuma jardiniere with matching stand, 3ft. high. $1,125 £500

An attractive Satsuma double gourd vase, painted with fans, 13.5cm. high, mid 19th century. $1,300 £580

A fine 19th century Satsuma bulbous koro and pierced dome cover. $1,685 £750

19th century Satsuma figure of a school girl, 72.5cm. high. $3,600 £1,60

Sevres hard paste cup and ucer, circa 1870.
$295 £130

One of a pair of 19th century Sevres porcelain circular shallow dishes, 9½in. diam. $660 £295

19th century Sevres gilt metal mounted rose pompadour ground pot pourri vase and cover, 29cm. high. $900 £400

Large Sevres pattern trembleuse cup, cover and stand. $1,350 £600

ODE

ode cup and saucer, pattn 967, circa 1810.
$45 £20

Spode two-handled cylindrical vase. $400 £180

Spode blue and white meat dish with sporting print.
$430 £190

Spode pastille burner and cover, circa 1830, 4in. high.
$540 £240

AFFORDSHIRE

ffordshire willow pattern p and saucer, circa 1860.
$15 £6

Staffordshire group of Napoleon and Albert, circa 1854, 14¼in. high. $180 £80

Staffordshire figure of a fox, 11cm. high, circa 1825. $315 £140

Staffordshire pottery group of King John signing the Magna Carta.
$360 £160

ffordshire silver lustre jug nsfer-printed in black with Molyneux/Cribb fight, a 1810, 14.5cm. high.
$385 £170

Obadiah Sherratt mantelpiece group, circa 1825-30, 13in. high. $540 £240

Staffordshire figure of Sir Robert Peel, circa 1850, 12¼in. high.
$890 £395

Staffordshire group of The Victory, modelled as an English sailor and a Turkish and French soldier.
$2,140 £950

STONEWARE

19th century stoneware quart jug with embossed scenic decoration. $80 £35

One of a pair of 19th century Bizan stoneware birds, 8½in. high. $240 £105

Victorian Gothic castle candleholder of glazed stoneware, 11½in. high. $240 £105

Stoneware urn, circa 186 36in. high. $450 £200

SUNDERLAND

Small early 19th century copper lustre mug depicting a coastal scene. $90 £40

Mid 19th century Sunderland lustre frog mug. $125 £55

Sunderland lustre jug, circa 1840, 7¼in. high. $250 £110

Rare jug of ovoid form, with pink lustre neck, probably Sunderland, about 1815. $955 £42

SWANSEA

Dillwyn & Co. Swansea plate, circa 1814, 9in. diam. $100 £45

Swansea inkwell, 4in. diam., 1814-22. $720 £320

Swansea Mandarin plate, transfer-printed and painted in famille rose. $720 £320

Swansea tureen, cover an stand, 7in. diam., 1814-2 $785 £3

Swansea teacup and saucer with floral decoration. $1,035 £460

Swansea plate of Burdett Coutts type, 9in. diam., 1814-22. $1,080 £480

Swansea inkwell, cover and liner, 5¼in. diam., 1814-22. $1,400 £625

Swansea 'bisque' ram 4¼in. long, 1817-21. $3,040 £1,35

edgwood earthenware bust Minerva, 17½in. high, mid th century. $540 £240

An early 19th century Wedgwood 'Rosso Antico' wine cooler of barrel shape, 9in. high. $585 £260

19th century Wedgwood blue and white jasperware pot pourri vase, 14in. high. $640 £285

19th century Wedgwood blue jasper plate with nine medallions, 12¾in. diam. $665 £295

edgwood creamware cruet ith five containers, circa 810, 17cm. wide. $720 £320

Wedgwood 'ornithological' teacup, coffee cup and saucer, 1812-22. $890 £395

Wedgwood three-colour jasper-dip cup and saucer, 1869, 5¾in. diam. $990 £440

Wedgwood and Bentley porphry ewer, 11in. high. $2,025 £900

ORCESTER

One of a pair of Grainger sauce tureens, circa 1810. $250 £110

One of a pair of Flight, Barr & Barr claret ground plates, circa 1820, 22.5cm. diam. $270 £120

Chamberlain Worcester figure of one of the Rainer Brothers, 6in. high, about 1830. $340 £150

Worcester teapot marked Flight, Barr & Barr, 1807-13. $450 £200

e of a pair of Worcester trepieces, 11¾in. high, a 1845. $485 £215

Pair of Worcester green vases, 1870, 10in. high. $1,430 £635

Grainger, Lee & Co. part dinner service, twenty-four pieces, 1812-20. $2,080 £925

One of a pair of Worcester Flight, Barr & Barr period lidded vases, 11in. high. $3,960 £1,760

Ornate French bracket clock with ormolu decoration. $330 £145

Mahogany bracket clock by F. J. Dent, London, 18in. high, circa 1840. $520 £230

A George IV mahogany bracket clock, 1ft.3½in. high. $980 £435

Early 19th century bracket clock by J. Harper, London. $1,080 £480

William IV mahogany bracket clock, dial inscribed Taylor & Son, Bristol, 19in. high. $1,150 £510

Regency ebonised striking bracket clock, signed Moncas, Liverpool, 18½in. high. $1,215 £540

Early 19th century ebonised lancet top bracket clock by Grant, London. $1,300 £580

Early 19th century bracket clock by P. Grimalde. $1,350 £600

English Regency bracket clock in mahogany case, 20in. high. $1,465 £650

Late George III mahogany bracket clock by Lautier, 10¼in. high. $1,680 £745

19th century bracket clock in mahogany case by Geo. Sharpe. $1,750 £780

19th century mahogany bracket clock in Turkish style, 27¾in. tall. $2,700 £1,200

Late George III striking bracket clock by Thos. Sutton, Maidstone, 15in. high. $2,900 £1,300

19th century bracket clock by Robert Simpson, London. $3,000 £1,350

19th century Japanese brass striking bracket clock, 165mm. high. $3,940 £1,750

Early 19th century mahogany musical bracket clock by J. & S. Farr, Bristol, 25in. high. $5,400 £2,400

Gilt metal striking carriage clock by Paul Garnier, Paris, 5in. high. $1,080 £480

19th century French gilt brass carriage clock by J. Soldarno. $1,465 £650

Small enamel mounted carriage timepiece, 3½in. high, in a red travelling case. $1,645 £730

Elaborate gilt metal striking carriage clock, 8¼in. high. $1,735 £770

Carriage clock by Bolviller Paris, 6½in. high. $1,755 £780

A French timepiece carriage clock, 9½in. high. $1,980 £880

Gilt metal timepiece carriage clock by J. McCabe, London, circa 1840, 4½in. high. $2,025 £900

Early 19th century travelling clock by Gordon of London, 9in. high. $2,200 £975

Repeat alarm carriage clock in a gorge case by Charles Frodsham & Co., Paris, circa 1875. $2,205 £980

19th century gilt brass and enamel mounted carriage clock, 6in. high. $2,590 £1,150

A polychrome enamel mounted alarm carriage clock by Leroy et Fils, Paris, 5¾in. high. $3,150 £1,400

Multi-piece carriage clock, London, 1841, 14cm. high, movement signed Parkinson & Frodsham. $3,825 £1,700

Biedermeier grande sonnerie alarm travelling clock, 9in. high. $4,275 £1,900

An enamel mounted grande sonnerie alarm carriage clock, 6½in. high. $5,965 £2,650

An English repeater carriage clock by James McCabe, 6¾in. high. $8,325 £3,700

Small ebony veneered carriage clock by Vulliamy, London, circa 1840, 6½in. high. $14,650 £6,500

29

Mid 19th century black marble, onyx and bronze clock garniture. $520 £230

Gilt bronze clock garniture, circa 1870, 16¾in. high. $540 £240

Late 19th century garniture of blue glass, clock by J. Leemans, Brussels $1,035 £46•

A Berlin clock garniture, the white enamel dial enclosed in a rococo case, 25.5cm. high, 1849-70. $1,125 £500

Ormolu bronze and marble clock garniture, by Briscard a Paris, 1870's, clock 18in. high. $1,300 £580

Mid 19th century garniture de che• inee of Vienna porcelain. $1,350 £60•

Brass and electrotype clock garniture, circa 1870. $1,350 £600

19th century garniture de cheminee, 52cm. high. $1,825 £815

Dresden garniture de cheminee, clo• 23in. high, candelabra 22in. high. $2,700 £1,20•

Composed white marble and ormolu clock garniture, circa 1870, clock 24½in. high. $4,500 £2,000

Fine Christofle cloisonne enamel clock garniture, 1874, clock 16¼in. high. $4,500 £2,000

Mid 19th century Sevres orm• mounted rose-pompadour clo• garniture. $8,100 £3,60•

19th century
ogany drum
l longcase clock
. Jeffrey.
$585 £260

Early 19th century
thirty-hour oak
cased grandfather
clock.$745 £330

Oak cased grand-
father clock, 80in.
high, circa 1800.
$775 £345

Early 19th century
oak cased grand-
father clock with
enamel dial.
$800 £355

Early 19th century
inlaid longcase
clock by James
Blaik, Peterhead.
$845 £375

rge IV' maho-
longcase clock,
1825, 97in.
$1,120 £520

Mahogany longcase
clock by Jn. & Wm.
Mitchell, Glasgow,
mid 19th century,
83in. high.
$1,285 £570

Mahogany longcase
clock, circa 1830,
93in. high.
$1,350 £600

Early 19th century
mahogany longcase
clock by Daniel
Brown, Glasgow,
7ft.3in. high.
$1,690 £750

Oak dead-beat long-
case clock with
brass dial, circa
1855, 92in. high.
$2,815 £1,250

h century oak
ed grandfather
ck with brass
.
2,970 £1,320

Boulle longcase clock
in waisted arched
case, mid 19th cen-
tury, 81½in. high.
$8,100 £3,600

Mid 19th century
French mahogany
equation of time
longcase clock, 6ft.
1in. high.
$8,100 £3,600

19th century
French pedestal
clock.
$9,000 £4,000

Early 19th century
mahogany French
longcase regulator
timepiece.
$11,250 £5,000

31

19th century American mantel clock in rosewood case. $55 £25

Victorian black marble mantel clock with brass fittings. $100 £45

Victorian oak cased mantel clock with drawer in the base. $250 £110

19th century clock with striking movement in a brass and ormolu case. $250 £11

Victorian spelter mantel clock depicting an artist, 1ft.8in. high.$340 £150

19th century French marble pillar clock. $400 £180

Bronze mantel clock, dial with Roman numerals, circa 1860, 9½in. high. $450 £200

George III ebonised mantel clock by Paterson, Edinburgh. $450 £20

Mid 19th century gilt bronze mantel clock, 11½in. high.$475 £210

An 'Hours Clock' by John Bell, 1851, in gilt on repousse copper. $500 £225

19th century marquetry cased mantel clock and stand. $560 £250

Early Martin Brothers clock case, 10½in. high, dated 10-74. $600 £26

Gilt bronze mantel clock, circa 1840, 16in. high. $620 £275

Gilt and silvered bronze mantel clock, circa 1870, movement signed Deniere a Paris, 18¼in. high. $790 £350

Mid 19th century boulle mantel clock, signed Fearn a Paris, 10½in. high. $790 £350

Charles X gilt bronze mantel clock with outside count wheel, circa 1830, 14in. high. $900 £40

ond Empire gilt and nze mantel clock, cir-860, 10in. high.
$925 £410

Red and black marble perpetual calendar mantel clock, circa 1860, 17½in. high. $1,125 £500

Early 19th century Directoire marble and ormolu mounted mantel clock, 22in. high. $1,510 £670

19th century Dresden cased mantel clock, 11½in. wide. $1,690 £750

Chinese rosewood table ck and stand, with mel dial and gilt sur-nd, circa 1800.
$1,755 £780

19th century boulle mantel clock with ormolu mounts. $1,800 £800

19th century French mantel clock, 28in. high.
$2,475 £1,100

A two-faced mahogany ship's clock by Litherland Davies & Co., Liverpool, circa 1840.
$2,815 £1,250

19th century malachite nted ormolu and silvered al mantel clock, 7½in.
$2,925 £1,300

Early 19th century French ormolu mantel clock, 16in. high. $3,600 £1,600

Mid 19th century table clock by Thomas Cole, 6in. high.
$3,600 £1,600

Large Louis XV gilt bronze mantel clock, dial signed Monbro Aine a Paris, circa 1840, 35½in. high.
$5,625 £2,500

century lyre clock in elain case, movement inable. $6,300 £2,800

Shelf clock by Aaron Willard in inlaid mahogany case, circa 1820. $10,575 £4,700

19th century Sevres and ormolu clock, 32in. high by 28in. long.
$13,000 £5,750

Early 19th century ormolu mounted Blue John clock by A. R. Simons of Paris.
$27,000 £12,000

33

An original Victorian skeleton timepiece, circa 1860. $730 £325

Skeleton timepiece with brass chapter ring, 10¾in. high. $950 £425

Skeleton clock by Hatfield & Hall, Manchester, 12½in. high. $1,400 £625

Skeleton timepiece by Barrauds, London, 1ft. 3in. high. $1,690 £750

Skeleton clock by Smith & Sons, Clerkenwell, 1ft. 4½in. high.$2,250 £1,000

Unusual timepiece skeleton clock, 20in. high, with glass dome. $2,700 £1,200

Large English striking skeleton clock, 22in. high. $2,925 £1,300

An early 19th century skeleton clock of 'rafter' construction. $3,265 £1,450

Rare chiming calendar skeleton clock, 1ft.7in. high. $4,050 £1,800

A long duration Dutch skeleton clock, 2ft.5in. high. $4,500 £2,000

English brass chiming skeleton clock, 20in. high. $5,400 £2,400

Brass cathedral skeleton clock signed C. Fiedemann, Liverpool. $5,625 £2,500

Early skeleton clock by Hubert Sarton, 1ft.5½in. high. $8,550 £3,800

Fine skeleton clock by James Condliff, Liverpool, 20½in. high, with glass dome. $8,550 £3,800

A chiming skeleton clock by James Condliff, Liverpool, dated 1860, 2ft.1in. high, sold with a glass dome. $22,500 £10,000

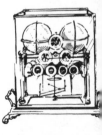

Astronomical skeleton clock by James Gorham, 19th century. $45,000 £20,000

It metal wall clock, circa
50, 20¾in. high.
$225 £100

Victorian papier mache wall
clock by E. Fixary.
$315 £140

19th century mahogany wall
clock with enamel dial by
Johnson, York. $385 £170

19th century oak cased
wall clock with ormolu
decoration. $450 £200

9th century French wall
ock with porcelain face
d painted surround.
$495 £220

Antique rosewood cased wall
clock, circa 1840, 23in. high.
$505 £225

Tavern wall clock in oak case,
circa 1850, 56in. high.
$540 £240

Mid 19th century mahogany
wall timepiece, dial signed
Robt. Mack, Clerkenwell,
16in. high. $565 £250

id 19th century Viennese
gulator clock with ebon-
ed case, 48in. high.
$810 £360

Gilt bronze cartel clock
with outside count wheel,
17in. high, circa 1870.
$945 £420

An unusual musical picture
clock depicting the Houses
of Parliament, circa 1870.
$945 £420

'Louis XV' gilt bronze cartel
clock, signed Veuvray Freres,
circa 1860, 20in. high.
$1,125 £500

e 18th/early 19th century
nch gilt metal repeating
l clock by Perache, Paris,
n. high. $1,485 £660

'Louis XVI' gilt bronze cartel clock, dial signed Paris,
circa 1870, 33in. high.
$1,845 £820

Oak observatory wall regulator by T. Cooke & Sons,
4ft.7in. high.
$2,925 £1,300

Early 19th century Viennese
walnut grande sonnerie wall
clock, 42in. high.
$9,000 £4,000

35

19th century gold detached lever watch by Morris Tobias, 50mm. diameter. $610 £270

Gold lever watch by F. B. Adams of London, 1835, 43mm. diam. $645 £285

Gold verge watch by Moon & Son, London, hallmarked 1812, 46mm. diam. $700 £310

Gold cylinder watch by James Tregent, London, circa 1800, 54mm. diam. $790 £350

Gold and enamel cylinder watch by Bautte & Co., Paris, 19th century, 36mm. diam. $1,035 £460

Gold cylinder watch by Rentzch of London, hall-marked 1826, 45mm. diam. $1,160 £515

Gold and turquoise set cylinder watch by Grant, London, 1819, 44mm. diam. $1,200 £530

A gold duplex watch by James McCabe, London, 1829, 50mm. diam. $1,240 £550

Early 19th century pair cased key wound verge watch by Charles Cabrier, London. $1,755 £780

Multi-colour gold verge watch by Horne & Ashe, London, 1809, 47mm. diam. $2,200 £980

Small gold and turquoise set verge watch by Moulinie Bautte & Moynier, Geneva, circa 1830, 27mm. diam. $2,365, £1,050

Gold and enamel pair cased verge watch by George Prior, London, 1815, 51mm. diam. $4,500 £2,000

Gold pair cased pocket chronometer by Thom. Earnshaw, 1801, 56mm. diam. $6,075 £2,700

Gold and pearl set verge watch, in the form of a basket, by Chevalier & Cochet, circa 1800, 34mm. long. $7,650 £3,400

Early 19th century gold and enamel quarter repeating musical watch for the Chinese market by Bovet, 64mm. diam. $19,125 £8,500

19th century gold cased two barrel lever watch by Bregue 52mm. diam. $56,250 £25,000

square onyx jardiniere
th cloisonne enamel
ounts, 10in. wide.
$450 £200

One of a pair of 19th century
ormolu mounted cloisonne
enamel vases. $755 £335

Early 19th century clois-
onne enamel incense
burner. $755 £335

Japanese cloisonne plate,
circa 1870, 18in. diam.
$785 £350

th century cloisonne
cense burner, Qianlong,
.6cm. high.$920 £410

One of a pair of clois-
onne Buddhist lions,
8in. high.$1,070 £475

One of a pair of 19th century Chinese cloisonne,
elephant shaped, incense
burners, 5½in. high.
$1,090 £485

One of a pair of early 19th
century cloisonne vases,
13½in. high.$1,180 £525

rly 19th century ewer
d cover in cloisonne,
½in. high.$1,295 £575

Chinese cloisonne covered
bowl, 14½in. diam.
$1,405 £625

A pair of Chinese clois-
onne enamel cranes.
$1,465 £650

One of a pair of cloisonne
vases, royal blue on powder
blue, circa 1860.
$2,250 £1,000

ge 19th century Japan-
cloisonne enamel dish,
n. diam.$2,250 £1,000

One of a pair of cloisonne
bulls, in turquoise, blue
and red, 9in. long, 6½in.
high. $2,815 £1,250

A fine Japanese cloisonne
enamel vase, 3ft. high.
$3,150 £1,400

Russian silver gilt and cloisonne enamel casket, 5in.
wide. $4,500 £2,000

Victorian brass trivet
with screw-on legs.
$35 £15

Horse brass, circa 1870.
$45 £20

Brass chamber stick with
a drip pan. $55 £25

Thick brass flat iron
stand, circa 1850, 11i
long. $63 £28

Solid brass pipe stopper,
circa 1830, 1½in. high.
$65 £29

One of a pair of unusual
brass and copper shaving
mugs. $75 £35

Georgian brass goffering
iron, circa 1835.
$90 £40

19th century copper
jelly mould. $90 £40

Victorian copper and brass
kettle. $100 £45

19th century muffin sel-
ler's handbell, 10in. high,
in perfect condition.
$108 £48

Circular brass tripod
candle reflector, circa
1800, 4½in. diam.
$105 £49

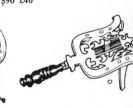

Early 19th century brass
lyre-shaped trivet with
wooden handle.
$112 £50

French fireman's brass
helmet. $112 £50

Small Victorian copper
kettle with brass mounted
wooden handle. $112 £50

A set of brass fire imple-
ments. $125 £55

Antique brass loving cup v
handles copper riveted to
body, circa 1850, 9in. hig
$125 £

Early 19th century cylindrical covered copper urn with brass spigot.
$135 £60

A large solid copper 19th century wash boiler, 20in. diam. $170 £75

19th century cast brass bracket with original hanging bell, 14in. high.
$176 £78

Antique copper coal-helmet. $180 £80

9th century copper preserve n with two handles, circa 40, 13¾in. diam.
$192 £85

Engraved brass and copper warming pan, circa 1850, 40in. long.
$190 £85

One gallon copper spirit measure, dovetail seams, circa 1850. $225 £100

One of a pair of brass candelabra, circa 1870, 18¼in. high. $245 £110

Cast and wrought iron footman, circa 1820, 12in. long. $315 £140

Mid 19th century copper salt barrel, 2ft.6in. high.
$325 £145

Brass standard measure, circa 1820. $335 £150

19th century brass ritual water ewer from Borneo, 11in. long. $370 £165

d 19th century copper ovar, 45cm. high.
$440 £190

One of a pair of mid 19th century English brass milk churns, 17in. high.
$1,380 £600

Regency brass and cast iron fireplace and matching fender.
$1,460 £650

One of a set of twelve cylindrical brass measures, from 5 gallons to ¼ gill.
$4,730 £2,200

CORKSCREWS

Victorian corkscrew with horn handle and brush, about 1860. $33 £15

Fine 19th century iron corkscrew with brush handle. $55 £25

19th century wine taster's tap screw with brush handle. $100 £45

Victorian brass and ivory corkscrew. $180 £80

Fine 19th century bar corkscrew, cast iron with round knob wooden handle, 9in. high. $215 £95

Unusual brass Victorian corkscrew. $370 £165

Steel rack and pinion hand corking device, 6¼in. high. $675 £300

Mid 19th century rare bro corkscrew, possibly Frenc $3,150 £1,4

COSTUME

Large chain point collar with scallop edge, circa 1840. $45 £20

Early 19th century green silk gown with leg of mutton sleeves, circa 1830. $125 £55

Court suit, circa 1860. $130 £60

Hand woven linen smoc frock or round frock used by a shepherd. $225 £100

A pair of 19th century blonde Chantilly stockings with side lacings, 78cm. long. $250 £115

Pair of Queen Victoria's bloomers. $530 £235

Pair of late 18th/early century gent's black leather riding boots, now used as an umbrella stand. $540 £250

19th century lady's Imperial Court drag robe. $900 £400

Doll's house lady doll, 6in. tall, circa 1860. $70 £30

Doll's house doll of a man, 7in. high, circa 1860. $100 £45

French, late Victorian doll shaped rattle. $135 £60

Bisque headed lady doll, circa 1870, 11½in. tall. $350 £155

Dark-haired Parian doll with original dress, circa 1865, ½in. long. $350 £155

A carved and painted wooden doll, the face with painted blue eyes and stitched brows, the stuffed body with wooden arms, circa 1860, 31in. high. $385 £170

Rare mid 19th century bisque 'frozen Charlotte' doll, 5½in. tall. $595 £265

Poured wax doll stamped Frederic Aldis, 20in. high. $630 £280

Rare Biedermeier shoulder papier mache doll, 13in. high, circa 1825. $640 £285

Pedlar doll with papier mache head and moulded hair, 8in. high, circa 1840. $675 £300

French bisque swivel headed doll with composition body and glass eyes, 20in. tall. $900 £400

Dark-haired Parian doll, circa 1850. $990 £440

German shoulder china doll, 17¼in. high, circa 1860, with a baby. $1,350 £600

Rare mid 19th century Motschmann articulated china doll, 10in. high. $1,675 £745

Huret bisque doll, 17in. high, hands and body repaired, marked Paris 1867. $2,430 £1,050

Carved and turned wooden doll, early 19th century. $2,475 £1,100

DOLLS HOUSES

Small Victorian doll's house with a hinged front, 14in. high. $340 £150

A doll's wooden house in the form of a three-storey building, with nine rooms. $1,035 £460

A large, painted, doll's wooden house, the lower section with outside stair-case, 5ft.2in. high, 4ft. wide. $1,125 £500

Victorian doll's house, 2ft. 4in. high. $1,295 £575

Rare Regency painted wooden two-storey doll's house and stand, 3ft.1in. wide. $1,295 £575

A mid Victorian three-storey doll's house on stand, 3ft.5in. wide. $1,675 £745

Victorian doll's house, completely fitted with furniture.$2,700 £1,200

Fine mid Victorian doll's house, fully furnished, 3ft. 9in. wide.$2,810 £1,250

FANS

Bone framed hand-painted fan, circa 1860, 18in. wide. $80 £35

George IV period Brise fan, circa 1825, 6¼in. high. $110 £50

An interesting silk picture, depicti a beautifully illustrated fan, circa 1860. $135 £6

Early Victorian lady's fan with rose-wood sticks, circa 1840, 9in. high. $170 £75

19th century painted fan, on pierced and gilded mother-of-pearl sticks. $170 £75

Early French Brise fan, 1ft.6in. wi $270 £12

Mid 19th century French mother-of-pearl fan with gilt and painted sticks, 29cm. long. $540 £240

Good blond tortoiseshell fan E. A. S. Douglas, 13¾in. long. $955 £425

Italian uncut Gouache fan mou circa 1820, 3ft.7¾in. high. $1,460 £65

Victorian mahogany single
bed with panelled ends.
$280 £125

Regency mahogany fold-
ing campaign bed, 7ft.
4in. high. $450 £200

Victorian painted metal
bed. $745 £330

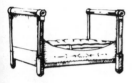

Empire mahogany single
bed with panelled head
and foot ends, 43¼in.
wide. $1,170 £520

Early 19th century Dutch
marquetry 'lit bateau', 3ft.
6in. wide. $1,295 £575

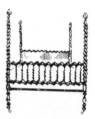

Victorian mahogany bed-
stead. $1,530 £680

Old English tent bed in
fruitwood with ogee shaped
canopy, 3ft.3in. wide.
          $1,575 £700

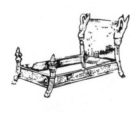

Giltwood and plaster bed,
19th century, 4ft. wide.
          $1,630 £725

Victorian mahogany double
bunk bed with stairs to the
upper tier. $1,630 £725

Solid satinwood poster bed,
foot posts reeded and gar-
landed, swags and decora-
tions carved from solid
posts, circa 1850, 5ft. wide,
8ft. high. $1,915 £850

19th century carved oak
half-tester bed.
          $5,400 £2,400

19th century Venetian giltwood bed, 78in. wide.
          $5,400 £2,400

BOOKCASES

19th century Victorian
mahogany bookcase with
glazed top, 230cm. high.
$360 £160

Carved oak bookcase,
1860's, 31in. wide.
$620 £275

Simulated rosewood book-
case, circa 1840, 104in.
wide. $900 £400

William IV mahogany l
rary bookcase with glaz
top, 111cm. wide.
$900 £40

19th century Continental
oak bookcase.
$1,465 £650

Carved Victorian bookcase
with open shelves.
$2,250 £1,000

Mahogany bookcase of
'Strawberry Hill' design,
48in. wide. $2,250 £1,000

William IV carved maho-
gany library bookcase, 84
wide. $2,250 £1,00

Mahogany bookcase with
recessed centre cornice,
circa 1830, 83¾in. wide.
$2,925 £1,300

Victorian mahogany break-
front library bookcase, 6ft.
1in. wide. $3,510 £1,560

Early 19th century
Regency mahogany revolv-
ing bookstand, 53in. high.
$3,600 £1,600

Late Regency breakfron
rosewood bookcase, 6ft.
6in. wide. $3,825 £1,7

George IV library book-
case, circa 1825, 6ft.2in.
wide. $3,940 £1,750

One of a pair of Regency
rosewood and brass inlaid
breakfront dwarf cabinets,
153cm. wide.
$4,165 £1,850

William IV pedestal book-
case in rosewood, 19½in.
high. $5,175 £2,300

Early 19th century libra
bookcase.$19,690 £8,7

44

Mid 19th century Continental mahogany cylinder bureau with bookshelves above. $675 £300

Early 19th century mahogany bureau bookcase with astragal glazed doors. $1,915 £850

Victorian bureau bookcase with glazed upper half. $1,970 £875

Georgian mahogany bureau bookcase, 42in. wide, circa 1820. $2,475 £1,100

Regency rosewood writing cabinet with a raised and painted mirror back. $2,815 £1,250

19th century floral marquetry bureau bookcase on cabriole legs. $2,815 £1,250

George III mahogany bureau bookcase with astragal glazed doors. $3,035 £1,350

Early 19th century walnut bureau bookcase with damaged veneer, 2ft.3in. wide. $3,035 £1,350

Early 19th century Chinese export lacquer bureau cabinet, 33in. wide. $3,265 £1,450

Regency kingwood bureau cabinet, inlaid on the front and sides. $3,375 £1,500

19th century mahogany and inlaid bureau bookcase, 38in. wide. $4,500 £2,000

Regency mahogany cylinder bureau bookcase, circa 1810, 3ft.8in. wide. $5,175 £2,300

9th century walnut bureau bookcase. $5,625 £2,500

Early 19th century Dutch marquetry bureau cabinet, 42in. wide. $6,750 £3,000

19th century marquetry bureau cabinet. $10,125 £4,500

Early 19th century Dutch marquetry bureau cabinet, with a bombe front. $13,500 £6,000

19th century stripped pine bureau on bracket feet, with brass handles, 3ft. wide. $505 £225

Louis XV style kingwood bureau de dame with brass gallery, 67cm. wide. $855 £380

Georgian mahogany bureau of good colour, 3ft. wide. $1,295 £575

19th century boulle bureau on cabriole legs. $1,350 £600

19th century Oriental carved teak bureau. $1,350 £600

Early 19th century German mahogany cylinder bureau, 3ft.6in. wide. $1,800 £800

19th century Dutch colonial block-fronted bureau, 92cm. wide. $1,970 £875

Mid 19th century Continental mahogany and painted cylinder bureau, 97cm. wide. $2,700 £1,200

19th century Dutch marquetry and walnut bombe-shaped lady's bureau, 90cm. wide. $3,375 £1,500

Mid 19th century French parquetry bureau, 28in. wide. $4,500 £2,000

19th century floral marquetry cylinder bureau with revolving top, 113cm. wide. $4,950 £2,200

North Italian marquetry bureau, circa 1830, 3ft.11in. wide. $6,750 £3,000

Viennese ormolu mounted mahogany cylinder bureau, circa 1825, 2ft.6in. wide. $7,200 £3,200

19th century writing desk with Swiss orchestral musical movement. $9,450 £4,200

A magnificent 19th century French mahogany tambour bureau with ormolu cupids, scrolls and foliage. $15,750 £7,000

French marquetry bureau a cylindre, 19th century 32½in. wide. $20,085 £9,250

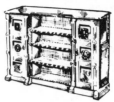

Victorian inlaid walnut wood cabinet surmounted with oval mirror, 24in. wide. $350 £155

Mid 19th century mahogany side cabinet, 40in. wide, with hinged top. $560 £250

Solid walnut side cabinet, mid 1870's, 73in. wide. $620 £275

Ebonised beechwood brass inlaid meuble d'appui, circa 1870, 42¾in. wide. $630 £280

19th century mahogany apothecary's cabinet. $655 £290

Victorian burr-walnut music cabinet, on turned legs, 41in. high. $810 £360

Victorian rosewood music cabinet. $900 £400

Early 19th century satinwood music cabinet, 1ft.7½in. wide. $900 £400

Oriental lacquer cabinet on stand. $900 £400

Mahogany collector's cabinet, 1860's, 49¾in. high. $925 £410

Satinwood bow-fronted side cabinet, 3ft.4in. wide. $1,195 £530

19th century walnut and tulipwood side cabinet, 33in. wide.$1,240 £550

19th century French parquetry cabinet with a marble top. $1,685 £750

19th century ornate carved walnut cabinet, 82cm. wide. $1,745 £775

Early 19th century Dutch colonial satinwood, ebony and coromandelwood cabinet, 4ft.7in. wide. $1,800 £800

Japanese black lacquer display cabinet on stand, 77cm. wide. $2,140 £950

CABINETS

Breakfront ebonised, gilt bronze and pietra dura side cabinet, with black slate top, circa 1850, 78in. wide. $2,140 £950

Victorian walnut cabinet complete with dental pliers. $2,135 £950

Regency simulated rosewood, satinwood and parcel gilt pedestal cabinet, 32¼in. wide. $2,475 £1,100

Carved oak side cabinet, with lower part made from a commode, circa 1850-80, 42in. wide. $3,265 £1,450

19th century French ebony and marquetry cabinet, 45¼in. wide. $5,515 £2,450

19th century Japanese Shibayama cabinet. $8,100 £3,600

Rare Godwin ebonised mahogany aesthetic cabinet, circa 1869, 96in. high. $14,625 £6,500

Fine Meissen and ebony cabinet, Dresden 1870. $45,000 £20,000

CANTERBURYS

A Victorian mahogany canterbury with fretted partitions. $420 £185

Victorian burr-walnut canterbury with shaped oval inlaid table top. $765 £340

Regency rosewood canterbury with drawer, 48cm. wide. $900 £400

19th century rosewood four division canterbury, 49cm. wide. $900 £400

Victorian burr-walnut canterbury. $900 £400

George III mahogany canterbury on slender turned tapered legs. $1,800 £800

Early 19th century mahogany canterbury 'whatnot' with bookrest top. $2,250 £1,000

Regency mahogany canterbury with eight divisions, 43in. wide. $3,265 £1,450

e of a pair of ebonised e chairs, 1870's. $145 £65

One of a pair of oak dining chairs by Alfred Water-house, 1870's. $340 £150

One of a set of four English mahogany side chairs with carved heads and armorial cartouches, 1870's. $430 £190

One of a set of four walnut chairs, circa 1830. $450 £200

e of a set of six 19th tury mahogany dining irs with shaped top s. $495 £220

One of a pair of Bettridge & Co. black papier mache boudoir chairs. $565 £250

One of a pair of Regency hall chairs with shell backs. $655 £290

One of a set of four 19th century rosewood dining chairs with scrolled balloon backs. $720 £320

e of a set of six maho-ny dining chairs, circa 40. $745 £330

One of a set of six Bieder-meier fruitwood chairs, circa 1830. $865 £385

One of a set of six walnut drawingroom chairs, 1860's. $1,125 £500

One of a set of six Regency ebonised dining chairs, Scottish. $1,170 £520

of a set of six German ogany veneered dining rs, 1840's. $1,240 £550

One of a set of six early 19th century French pro-vincial cherrywood dining chairs with rush seats. $1,365 £610

One of a set of four Dutch marquetry dining chairs, circa 1810. $1,690 £750

One of a set of twelve maho-gany dining chairs, 19th cen-tury. $12,375 £5,500

49

Victorian Abbotsford chair with needlework upholstery. $225 £100

19th century rosewood framed armchair with carved cresting rail. $450 £200

Military officer's convertible chair-bed in iron and brass, circa 1840-60. $565 £250

Mid Victorian upholstered walnut lady's chair with cabriole legs, 35in. high. $665 £29

Italian walnut crinoline chair, circa 1830. $675 £300

Victorian steel-framed rocking chair with leather upholstery. $565 £250

English walnut armchair with crested back and serpentine seat on cabriole legs, circa 1860. $745 £330

English walnut button-ba armchair with moulded frame and serpentine sea circa 1860. $880 £39

An early 19th century giltwood armchair carved in the Louis XV manner. $900 £400

One of a pair of Anglo-Indian ebony armchairs, mid 19th century. $900 £400

Charles X inlaid pollard-elm bergere, circa 1820. $990 £440

Early 19th century rose wood armchair, upholstered in leather. $1,690 £75

One of a pair of Regency mahogany bergeres with padded backs and leather seats, on X frames. $2,140 £950

One of a pair of Swedish giltwood bergeres with husk-carved arms, circa 1800. $3,150 £1,400

One of a pair of Regency mahogany bergeres with caned backs, sides and seats. $5,625 £2,500

American library armcha attributed to Duncan Phyfe, circa 1815. $33,750 £15,0

50

Mid 19th century English oak X-framed leather upholstered armchair.
$215 £95

child's chair, Russian, 50's, 26½in. high.
$90 £40

Victorian beechwood smoker's chair with saddle seat. $100 £45

Oak and elm 19th century spindleback chair with curved arms. $180 £80

Anglo-Indian ebony arm-chair, circa 1830, with caned back and seat.
$585 £260

rly 19th century Chippen-e style mahogany elbow air on ball and claw feet.
$340 £150

An Italian walnut and ivory Savonarola armchair, circa 1860. $395 £175

Mid 19th century walnut 'grotto' armchair.
$520 £230

Regency carved oak rail-back armchair.
$1,125 £500

orge IV caned mahogany rary chair, circa 1820.
$720 £320

Empire mahogany fauteuil with stuffed back, circa 1815. $865 £385

Empire mahogany armchair, circa 1810. $1,015 £450

th century Korean cinna-r lacquer and gilded open nchair with leather seat.
$1,350 £600

Mahogany elbow chair, probably Continental and early 19th century, with floral marquetry inlay.
$1,350 £600

Buffalo horn armchair by W. Friedrich, Texas.
$1,575 £700

German Regency beech-wood open armchair with caned back. $2,250 £1,000

Early 19th century mahogany chest on splay feet. $225 £100

Early 19th century mahogany bow-front chest of three long drawers. $505 £225

Victorian mahogany campaign chest of two halves with inset brass handles, 40in. wide. $520 £230

Mid 19th century painted chest of seven drawers, with a marble top. $540 £240

Small mahogany chest of drawers, 2ft.9in. wide, circa 1810. $640 £285

Mahogany Wellington chest of drawers, 1870's, 22¾in. wide. $640 £285

Quaint poker work chest of drawers, signed by Laura Allsop, 35in. wide x 32in. high, circa 1845. $675 £300

Biedermeier satinwood chest of drawers, circa 1825, 3ft. wide. $900 £400

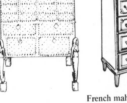

19th century Italian carved walnut chest, 5ft. wide. $1,000 £440

French mahogany chest of drawers of unusual design, ormolu mounts, 36in. wide, 33in. high, circa 1850. $1,015 £450

19th century Eastern inlaid teak chest supported by four mermaids. $1,105 £490

French mahogany chest of drawers with original ormolu mounts and handles, 38in. wide, circa 1850. $1,240 £55

Small antique walnut Wellington chest of seven drawers, 23in. wide. $1,395 £620

Regency period camphorwood secretaire military chest. $1,690 £750

Early 19th century Dutch marquetry bombe shaped chest of drawers, 37in. wide. $3,490 £1,550

Early 19th century French mahogany semainier with white marble top, 37in. wide. $3,600 £1,600

rge III mahogany tall-
with original handles,
in. wide.$1,240 £550

Mid 19th century Georgian
design mahogany bow-
fronted tallboy, 112cm.
wide. $1,300 £580

Early 19th century walnut
chest on chest, of small
proportions, 36in. wide.
                $1,915 £850

19th century oak and wal-
nut cabinet on chest,
heavily carved, 50in. wide.
        $2,700 £1,200

EST ON STANDS

arly 19th century walnut
est on stand. $630 £280

19th century carved oak
cabinet on stand, in the
French Gothic style.
        $1,015 £450

George III oak chest on
stand. $1,015 £450

Early 19th century simu-
lated walnut chest on stand,
2ft.8in. wide.$1,465 £650

IFFONIERS

ctorian rosewood chif-
nier, 45in. wide.
        $505 £225

Small Georgian mahogany
chiffonier, 40in. wide,
circa 1830. $565 £250

Victorian burr-walnut chiffonier with marble top,
48in. wide. $765 £340

Mid 19th century rosewood
chiffonier with two-tier
back, 45in. wide.
        $900 £400

ency chiffonier in rose-
od, circa 1820, 36in.
e. $1,180 £525

Regency mahogany chif-
fonier with scroll supports.
        $1,350 £600

Regency brass inlaid rosewood chiffonier, 2ft.9in.
wide, circa 1810.
        $3,490 £1,550

Late George III mahogany
chiffonier, circa 1800, 2ft.
3in. wide, with graduated
top. $4,950 £2,200

53

COMMODE CHESTS

19th century boxwood strung floral marquetry inlaid kingwood commode, 2ft.2in. wide. $810 £360

Biedermeier fruitwood commode with panelled ebonised frieze, circa 1820, 4ft. wide. $945 £420

Early 19th century French provincial kingwood petite commode, 41cm. high. $1,125 £500

19th century Adam sty demi-lune commode in and painted with scroll motifs, by Edwards & Roberts. $1,845 £820

An ornate French 19th century commode with ebonised ormolu mounting. $2,815 £1,250

Edwards & Roberts mid 19th century marble top Louis XVI style commode in rosewood, 80cm. wide. $3,150 £1,400

Mid 19th century ebonised and marquetry commode. $10,125 £4,500

Regency boulle commo en tombeau. $30,375 £13,50

COMMODES AND POT CUPBOARDS

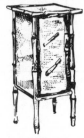

Victorian bamboo and cane pot cupboard. $65 £30

Victorian mahogany commode complete with liner. $80 £35

19th century French walnut pot cupboard on shaped legs. $135 £60

19th century mahoga lift-up commode wit' shaped apron. $170

Victorian mahogany pot cupboard with fluted sides. $225 £100

Mahogany bedside table, circa 1800, 31in. high, with slatted shelf. $370 £165

Unconverted night commode, circa 1800, 28in. high. $385 £170

One of a pair of Regency mahogany bedside cupboards, circa 1805, 1ft.4i wide. $1,575 £700

54

Inlaid bow-fronted corner display cupboard. $295 £130

Victorian carved oak corner cupboard with broken arch pediment. $450 £200

Walnut open corner cupboard, circa 1860, 72 x 29in. $765 £340

19th century French kingwood and walnut veneered encoignure, 28½in. wide. $900 £400

19th century Dutch floral marquetry corner cupboard. $965 £430

Walnut veneered early 19th century glazed corner cupboard. $1,195 £530

Early 19th century Georgian design standing mahogany corner cupboard, 120cm. wide. $1,620 £720

Mahogany Regency corner cupboard, 36in. wide, circa 1820. $1,685 £750

CRADLES

19th century Breton style cradle, with turned finials, 90cm. wide. $160 £70

19th century mahogany crib with carved end, 97cm. long. $245 £110

A Victorian brass crib. $340 £150

A 19th century Indian cradle. $340 £150

Regency caned mahogany cradle, 3ft.11in. high, circa 1820. $730 £325

George IV mahogany cradle, 3ft.1in. wide, circa 1825. $945 £420

Early 19th century parcel gilt mahogany cradle, 3ft. 11in. wide. $1,080 £480

Mid 19th century painted cradle, 38½in. long. $1,240 £550

55

CREDENZAS

Ebonised and burr-walnut side cabinet, 58in. wide, circa 1860. $520 £230

Mid 19th century walnut side cabinet, 67in. wide. $720 £320

19th century rosewood breakfro credenza with shaped back and ley twist columns. $1,465 £65

Burr-walnut side cabinet, 1860's, 72in. wide. $3,600 £1,600

19th century boulle and ormolu credenza, 7ft. wide.$4,500 £2,000

Mid Victorian walnut and marque side cabinet by Gillows. $13,500 £6,0

CUPBOARDS

Mahogany and oak linen press, 50in. wide. $600 £270

Biedermeier fruitwood cupboard, circa 1830, 3ft.8in. wide. $675 £300

19th century Flemish tridarn cupboard, 34in. wide. $845 £375

Bleached oak court cupboard, 57in. wide, circa 1860. $1,015 £450

19th century Colonial carved teak linen press, 48in. wide. $1,185 £525

19th century French carved oak cupboard on a stand, 48in. wide. $2,025 £900

19th century Flanders carved neo-renaissance cupboard in oak. $3,265 £1,450

Early 19th century Fren provincial cherrywood c board with shaped panel doors. $4,165 £1,85

nut Davenport writing e, circa 1870, 20¾in. e. $675 £300

Mid 19th century walnut Davenport, 32 x 23½in. $675 £300

Walnut Davenport, circa 1860, 37½in. wide, with central turned balustrade. $745 £330

Regency Davenport of mahogany surmounted by a letter tray, 76cm. wide. $765 £340

ewood Davenport, 0's, with leather-lined 20¾in. wide. $970 £430

Mahogany Davenport with pierced brass gallery, 33½in. wide, circa 1830. $1,015 £450

Victorian rosewood Davenport, with serpentine front, 53cm. wide. $1,095 £485

Victorian rosewood piano top Davenport, 25in. wide. $1,575 £700

ncy rosewood Daven- surmounted by a gallery, 17in. wide. $1,575 £700

Boulle Davenport with brass and gilt metal decoration, 21in. wide. $1,690 £750

Mid Victorian walnut Davenport with gallery top. $2,025 £900

William IV rosewood Davenport, circa 1830, 1ft.9in. wide. $2,250 £1,000

orian inlaid figured ut piano front nport desk, 23in. . $2,250 £1,000

Regency Davenport in mahogany, the side cupboard with four drawers and rare spring-operated secret compartment. $2,250 £1,000

A superb quality small Regency rosewood Davenport only 1ft.2in. wide. $3,375 £1,500

Davenport in rosewood with baluster gallery and sphinx-carved cupports. $3,600 £1,600

19th century mahogany display table with brass embellishments. $450 £200

Small walnut cabinet with gilt mounts, 30in. wide. $605 £270

Early 19th century ebonised display cabinet with brass string inlay. $1,125 £500

Biedermeier fruitwood play cabinet, 50½in. w $1,530 £6

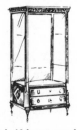   

Early 19th century mahogany vitrine, frieze with gilt bronze banding, 36in. wide. $1,620 £720

Breakfront walnut cabinet, raised on dwarf cabriole legs, circa 1850, 5ft. wide, 1ft.9in. deep, 4ft.6in. high. $1,685 £750

Burr-walnut display cabinet on stand, 1870's, 79 x 28½in. $1,745 £775

Mid 19th century Flen carved oak display cab 41½in. wide. $2,070 £92

Dutch marquetry display cabinet, circa 1840, 55in. wide. $2,475 £1,100

One of a pair of unusual 19th century satinwood china display cabinets, 14in. wide. $4,050 £1,800

19th century French rosewood and Vernis Martin vitrine, 57in. wide, with ormolu mounts. $4,950 £2,200

Dutch walnut and mar try display cabinet wit arched top, circa 1840 87in. high.$6,525 £2,9

19th century Japanese Shibayama display cabinet. $9,000 £4,000

19th century French kingwood vitrine, door panels painted in the Vernis Martin manner. $9,450 £4,200

Louis XV style kingwood display and writing cabinet, circa 1860.$11,250 £5,000

Mid 19th century Dutch quetry display cabinet, 4 9in. wide. $30,375 £13,

small Victorian stripped ine dresser base with haped brass handles, 4ft. ide. $315 £140

19th century German dresser with two drawers. $315 £140

Victorian carved oak dresser with pot board. $565 £250

19th century Jacobean style dresser, 4ft.7in. wide. $675 £300

mall 19th century stripped ne dresser with drawers d cupboards, 3ft.3in. de. $785 £350

Continental cupboard dresser, 47in. wide, circa 1840. $810 £360

Oak dresser with split baluster decoration, circa 1860, 59in. wide. $1,070 £475

Victorian 'Dog Kennel' dresser, circa 1850, 63in. wide. $1,295 £575

rly 19th century stripped e dresser with pot board. $1,350 £600

Early 19th century dresser and rack in honey coloured oak, 64in. wide. $1,800 £800

Early 19th century oak dresser with raised plate rack, 5ft.7in. wide. $2,925 £1,300

George III oak dresser, 6ft. 2in. wide, circa 1800. $3,710 £1,650

MB WAITERS

h century two-tier dumb er with turned central mn, 68cm. diam. $630 £280

19th century mahogany three-tier dumb waiter of Georgian design, 118cm. high. $790 £350

Regency period two-tier dumb waiter on splay feet with castors. $1,015 £450

Regency mahogany dumb waiter with brass gallery and reeded tripod base with claw castors. $1,350 £600

Mid 19th century mahogany pedestal desk, 36in. wide.
$450 £200

Late Georgian mahogany gentleman's kneehole desk, circa 1830, 36in. wide.
$600 £265

Victorian mahogany cylinder pedestal desk.
$990 £440

Mid 19th century carved oak pedestal desk, top w outset corners, 62in. wid
$1,080 £48

Rosewood kneehole specimen cabinet, 1840's, 58in. wide. $1,080 £480

Small oak kneehole desk with cupboard doors, 45in. wide.
$1,125 £500

Seddon style carved oak and decorated kneehole desk, circa 1860. $1,350 £600

19th century japanned pe stal pedestal desk, 3ft.10in. long.
$1,465 £65

19th century secretaire kneehole desk in mahogany, 3ft.1in. wide.
$1,350 £600

Carved walnut pedestal desk, 1860's, 46in. wide.
$1,620 £720

Early 19th century ebonised pedestal desk decorated with brass moulding, circa 1820. $1,690 £750

19th century walnut and kingwood, kidney-shape kneehole desk, the top lined with tooled leather
$4,500 £2,00

Late George III mahogany pedestal desk, circa 1810, 4ft.4in. wide.
$6,300 £2,800

'Louis XIV' boulle bureau mazarin, 48in. wide, circa 1850. $8,550 £3,800

Victorian oak pedestal desk by Thomas Knight.
$9,450 £4,200

Early 19th century ivor inlaid kneehole desk, 3 5in. wide.$22,500 £10

   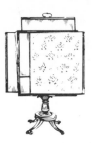

an brass firescreen with decoration. $100 £45

William IV mahogany pole screen, circa 1830, with later tapestry. $160 £70

Mid 19th century brass pole with beadwork screen, supported on ebonised base.$200 £90

Mahogany framed three-panel extending screen. $215 £95

light rosewood wool-irescreen, 1850's, 8½in. $295 £130

Mid 19th century rose-wood adjustable screen with tapestry, 36in. high. $290 £130

Walnut pole screen with circular embroidered panel, 60in. high, circa 1860. $400 £180

Mid 19th century oak fire-screen with numerous bevel glazed panels. $550 £240

firescreen, 1860's, gh. $675 £300

Victorian parlour firescreen, 4ft. high, in double-glazed glass case. $700 £310

Early 19th century rose-wood inlaid escritoire firescreen, 3ft.9in. $1,125 £500

Jennens & Bettridge papier mache firescreen, 41in. high, circa 1850. $1,125 £500

tury Chinese hard-reen with red and cquer.$1,150 £510

Walnut four-fold screen inset with oval embroidered reserves, 76in. tall, circa 1860. $3,600 £1,600

19th century Oriental padouk four-fold screen, 228cm. wide. $4,165 £1,850

Early 19th century six-leaf screen, 70½in. high. $6,750 £3,000

Victorian rosewood secretaire Wellington chest. $745 £330

Regency mahogany secretaire chest with ebony stringing. $900 £400

South German mahogany secretaire, 1840's, 39in. wide. $955 £425

Burr-chestnut secreta semanier with white marble top, 1870's, 2 wide. $1,015 £4

Georgian mahogany fallfront secretaire, circa 1835. $1,015 £450

Victorian oak secretaire cabinet, 36in. wide. $1,465 £650

19th century coromandel wood chest with a fitted secretaire drawer. $1,575 £700

George IV mahogany retaire cabinet, circa 1 3ft.6½in. wide. $1,575 £

A teak secretaire military chest, 30in. wide, circa 1820. $1,690 £750

Charles X mahogany secretaire, circa 1830, 3ft.3in. wide. $1,690 £750

Biedermeier mahogany secretaire, 3ft.9in. wide, circa 1820-40. $1,800 £800

Early 19th century Du mahogany secretaire. $3,940 £1

Satinwood secretaire a abattant, possibly Polish, circa 1820, 2ft.10in. wide. $4,500 £2,000

Serpentine kingwood and marquetry secretaire, circa 1870, 27½in. wide. $5,965 £2,650

19th century satinwood escritoire, 95cm. wide. $7,200 £3,200

Empire ormolu mou mahogany secretaire abattant, circa 1810, 2¼in. wide. $10,125 £4

century Burmese
d hardwood secre-
cabinet.
$1,170 £520

Victorian mahogany secre-
taire bookcase on turned
legs. $1,685 £750

Early 19th century maho-
gany secretaire bookcase
with satinwood interior,
3ft.9in. wide.
$1,825 £810

Dutch mahogany secre-
taire bookcase with carved
cresting, late 1840's,
40½in. wide.$2,205 £980

19th century Ameri-
ahogany writing
t, 4ft.2in. wide.
$2,250 £1,000

Early 19th century maho-
gany secretaire bookcase,
circa 1825, 32in. wide.
$2,925 £1,300

American figured mahogany
and satinwood lined cylinder secretaire bookcase,
4ft.1in. wide.
$2,925 £1,300

Secretaire bookcase of late
Regency period, with lat-
tice glazed doors of unusual design.$3,150 £1,400

Georgian secretaire
case in mahogany
astragal glazed doors.
$3,490 £1,550

Mahogany secretaire book-
case with gilt enrichments,
possibly Irish, circa 1835,
258cm. high.
$4,050 £1,800

Regency secretaire military
cabinet in burr-elm, circa
1820. $4,500 £2,000

Regency mahogany break-
front secretaire bookcase,
185cm. wide.
$4,500 £2,000

III mahogany secre-
est, 42in. wide.
$6,750 £3,000

Regency mahogany break-
front secretaire bookcase,
84in. wide. $8,440 £3,750

Regency mahogany bureau
cabinet with tambour cylinder cover, 4ft.4½in. wide.
$10,350 £4,600

George IV mahogany break-
front secretaire bookcase
by Gillow. $16,875 £7,500

Mid 19th century grained rosewood chaise longue. $450 £200

Victorian mahogany scroll end settee on turned legs. $495 £220

Scottish 'William IV' chaise lo with moulded frame and over scrolled ends, late 1830's, 78i $630 £2

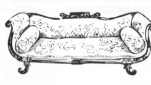

Regency couch in mahogany inlaid with ormolu. $675 £300

Regency painted settee, circa 1805, 6ft. 11in. wide. $820 £365

A carved oak hall settle, 56in. $900

Mid 19th century ebonised settee with button upholstered back and seat, 68in. wide, probably German. $945 £420

Walnut settee, 75in. long, circa 1860, with carved toprail. $990 £440

Burmese settee of serpentine s extensively carved and pierced $1,015 £

English walnut chaise longue, with button upholstered end and half back, circa 1860, 74¾in. long. $1,080 £480

Victorian walnut framed serpentine shaped settee, 183cm. wide. $1,188 £528

George IV mahogany settee, 1820, 6ft.1in. long. $1,395 £

Italian parcel gilt mahogany chaise longue, circa 1815, 5ft.9in. long. $2,225 £990

19th century ornate carved oak settle in French Renaissance style, 195cm. wide. $2,475 £1,100

Russian amboyna wood chaise lo with gilt enrichments. $15,750 £7,0

Victorian mahogany sideboard with cellarette drawer. $340 £150

Custom mahogany Jacobean style sideboard with carved gallery, 58in. wide. $385 £170

19th century inlaid mahogany sideboard with brass gallery. $450 £200

19th century rosewood board, 68 x 66in. $450 £200

A walnut and burr-walnut open sideboard, the canted corners held by female caryatids, 58in. wide, circa 1850. $675 £300

Small English ebonised mahogany sideboard. $730 £325

ncy mahogany sideboard, richly red, 4ft.9in. wide. $790 £350

Early Victorian mahogany sideboard, mirror back carved with acanthus, fruit and 'C' scrolls, 84½in. wide. $855 £380

A large, Regency, crossbanded mahogany sideboard on turned legs. $900 £400

century painted satinwood ard. $1,070 £475

Early 19th century mahogany sideboard on tapered legs with spade feet. $1,090 £485

William IV mahogany and crossbanded bow-front sideboard, 155cm. wide. $1,350 £600

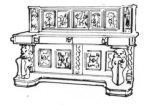

9th century oak sideboard, heavily 90in. wide. $2,025 £900

Late Georgian mahogany bow-fronted small sideboard. $2,700 £1,200

Large carved oak sideboard, 19th century, Flemish, 8ft.2in. long. $6,190 £2,750

STANDS

Victorian mahogany towel rail on twist supports. $45 £20

19th century mahogany easel. $110 £50

Victorian mahogany hat stand in the Gothic manner. $225 £100

Mid 19th century wa music stand with dou rests. $315 £1

Small Regency hall table. $395 £175

One of a pair of Italian ebony and majolica plant stands. $520 £230

19th century mahogany music stand with hinged easel, 52cm. wide. $630 £280

One of a pair of marq try etageres, circa 187 30¼in. high. $675 £3

Heavily carved oak hall stand with lifting lidded seat. $835 £370

Regency William IV double music stand in rosewood. $900 £400

Georgian duet stand. $955 £425

One of a pair of red a green tortoiseshell bo centre pedestals, circa 1830. $1,035 £46

Early Victorian mahogany folio rack. $1,240 £550

Mid 19th century japanned jardiniere, 2ft.1in. wide. $1,350 £600

One of a pair of 19th century Regency satinwood music stands, 45in. high. $4,050 £1,800

George III mahogany ing table, 24in. wide. $5,060 £2

66

circular beadwork
ool with mahogany
me. $45 £20

19th century mahogany
framed stool. $45 £20

Victorian walnut framed foot-
stool with a padded woolwork
top, circa 1850. $80 £35

George III style dressing
stool with needlework top,
45cm. wide. $90 £40

torian walnut stool with
inal castors, circa 1850.
                   $100 £45

Victorian wind-up piano
stool, upholstered in Dralon.
                   $135 £60

An unusual Victorian foot-
stool made from elk's feet
with an oak top.$195 £75

A Danish marquetry stool,
2ft.3in. wide, circa 1820.
                   $340 £150

liam IV mahogany
p chair with adjust-
e seat. $480 £210

Second Empire mahogany
stool with drop-in seat,
19½in. square, circa 1870.
                   $765 £340

Early Victorian rosewood,
gros point stool.
                   $785 £350

Rare Wedgwood spin-
ette stool, 18in. high.
                   $1,460 £650

nid 19th century brass
ame stool, 2ft.5in.
e. $3,375 £1,500

Early 19th century window
seat in the manner of
Duncan Phyfe.
            $3,940 £1,750

A superb Regency stool
with carved gilt rope feet
            $4,500 £2,000

Regency mahogany and
parcel gilt stool, circa 1810,
1ft.10½in. wide.
            $5,175 £2,300

English cast iron seat with two chairs decorated in the fern pattern, about 1870-80, seat 4ft.6in. wide, chair 2ft. wide. $900 £400

Button upholstered walnut drawingroom suite, 1860's. $1,935 £860

Early 19th century Empire style three-piece suite. $3,375 £1,500

Very fine mid Victorian walnut salon suite. $4,950 £2,200

liam IV mahogany fold-
r tea table supported
octagonal column, 91cm.
e. $180 £80

19th century inlaid maho-
gany and flap-over card
table. $360 £160

Rosewood card table,
1840's, 36in. wide.
$540 £240

William IV mahogany tea
table on concave sided
base with scroll feet, 40½in.
wide, circa 1835.
$540 £240

rr-walnut card table,
60's, 35in. wide.
$700 £310

19th century mahogany
fold-over top card table.
$845 £375

Victorian rosewood fold-over
card table. $865 £385

Regency brass inlaid burr-
elm card table, circa 1820,
3ft.2in. wide.$945 £420

h Empire rosewood
walnut folding top
table, 2ft.9½in.
. $1,685 £750

Regency rosewood tea
table on four concave
shaped legs, 2ft.11½in.
wide. $2,700 £1,200

Regency brass inlaid card
table, circa 1815, 2ft.11½in.
wide, in mahogany with
rosewood crossbanding.
$2,925 £1,300

One of a pair of mid 19th
century English folding
card tables.
$12,375 £5,500

SOL

orian cast iron consol
with marble top.
$280 £125

William IV consol table in
rosewood, 3ft.2in. wide.
$1,015 £450

Mid 19th century rosewood
consol table, one of a pair,
48in. wide. $1,125 £500

Regency giltwood consol
table with Sicilian jasper
top, 35¾in. wide.
$7,200 £3,200

Victorian mahogany centre table, 3ft. wide, on cabriole legs. $370 £165

Walnut centre table, circa 1870, 48½in. wide.
$450 £200

Small Victorian mahogany centre table on a platform base with claw feet.
$450 £200

Round walnut dining table with carved legs and stretchers, sold with six matching chairs. $665 £295

Circular rosewood Oriental carved table. $810 £360

Burr-walnut circular breakfast table, 1860's, 48in. diam. $1,125 £500

Rosewood circular breakfast table, 64in. diam., 1830's. $1,170 £520

Mid 19th century Batavian ebony centre table, 47in. diam. $1,390 £620

19th century coromandel breakfast table, 4ft. diam.
$1,620 £720

Mahogany drum table, circa 1840, 3ft.10in. diam. $1,635 £725

North German or Russian mahogany centre table, circa 1820, 2ft.6½in. square. $2,025 £900

19th century scarlet boulle and ebonised centre table
$2,140 £95

Victorian inlaid walnut table with carved scrolled supports and legs.
$3,825 £1,700

Regency zebra wood breakfast table with mahogany crossbanding, 4ft.8in. x 3ft.6in. $5,625 £2,500

George III mahogany breakfast table with tip-up top, 60in. wide. $6,075 £2,700

Circular Victorian tilt-top table in walnut marquetry
$6,300 £2,8

orian mahogany dress-
able. $315 £140

19th century Sheraton
style satinwood veneered
dressing table, 21in. wide.
                    $330 £145

Victorian chest of drawers
with fitted top drawer,
marble top and toilet mirror. $955 £425

Mid 19th century walnut
and ormolu mounted toilet
table, signed Tahn of Paris,
53cm. wide. $1,240 £550

rge III mahogany dress-
table by Gillow of Lan-
er, circa 1805, 3ft.6in.
e. $2,025 £900

19th century amboyna
and marquetry dressing
table, 37in. wide.
            $2,250 £1,000

Early Victorian bird's eye
maple and marquetry
kneehole dressing table
and matching toilet mirror,
60in. wide. $3,940 £1,750

Empire mahogany dress-
ing table with arched swing
mirror, 30in. wide.
            $4,050 £1,800

DP-LEAF TABLES

try made oak drop-leaf
, circa 1820.$225 £100

Victorian carved oak gateleg table on barley twist
supports. $225 £100

19th century mahogany
drop-flap table on pad
feet. $340 £150

Early 19th century maho-
gany breakfast table on
quadruple sabre leg base.
                    $790 £350

ian parquetry top
and walnut writ-
table, 105cm.
e. $1,035 £460

George III mahogany din-
ing table, circa 1810.
            $1,125 £500

William IV mahogany din-
ing table, 1830's, 48in.
wide. $1,690 £750

Regency mahogany extend-
ing dining table, circa 1815,
8ft.4in. long.$3,220 £1,430

19th century mahogany Wake's table with double gateleg action. $900 £400

William IV rosewood library table, 1830's, 54in. wide. $520 £230

Walnut centre table, circa 1860, 48i wide. $540 £2

Mid 19th century American pitch pine refectory table, 96½in. long. $745 £330

Mid 19th century mahogany expanding dining table, on ten turned legs. $1,035 £460

Mahogany dining table with cro banded top, circa 1830. $1,125 £50

Mid 19th century mahogany centre table, 51½in. wide. $1,440 £640

Carved rosewood library table. $1,465 £650

Mid 19th century walnut centre ta 72in. long. $1,630 £7.

Solid mahogany dining table which makes two breakfast tables, circa 1830. $1,690 £750

Mid 19th century provincial oak table, 5ft.6½in. long. $1,800 £800

Mahogany dining table with latti underframing, George IV, circa 1825, 7ft.6in. x 4ft.5in. $1,915 £850

Early 19th century mahogany pedestal dining table, extending to 12ft., with extra pedestal. $3,600 £1,600

George III mahogany three pedestal table, 51 x 152in. extended. $4,500 £2,000

Fine Regency three pedestal din table, 59¼in. wide. $12,375 £5,5

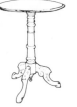

th century mahogany
casional table on tripod
se. $100 £45

19th century Burmese teak
occasional table, legs in the
form of elephants' heads.
$135 £60

Victorian walnut circular
occasional table on a carved
tripod base. $170 £75

19th century lacquered
nest of tables. $215 £95

id 19th century French
arquetry side table of
ngwood, 54cm. wide.
$270 £120

19th century rosewood
centre table on a stretcher
base. $295 £130

Victorian walnut turtle top
table with white marble
top. $300 £135

19th century mahogany
galleried table.
$460 £205

ardwood camel, 28in.
gh, which supports a
rved coffee table.
$540 £240

Victorian walnut table with
round marble top inlaid
with intricate patterns.
$565 £250

Octagonal walnut inlaid
table, circa 1840, 28in.
high. $745 £330

Regency rosewood centre
table with circular top,
24in. diam., inset with 18th
century Imari dish.
$955 £425

19th century Italian
aised blackamoor table
marble top, 20½in.
. $1,485 £660

Boulle jardiniere with zinc
container on cabriole legs,
1860's, 31½in. wide.
$1,620 £720

Kingwood and Sevres eta-
gere, top inset with porcelain dish, 1870's, 29in.
high. $4,725 £2,100

Dutch marquetry centre
table, circa 1830, with
late 17th century panels.
$10,125 £4,500

73

PEMBROKE TABLES

George III mahogany Pembroke table crossbanded in satinwood, 114cm. wide.
$295 £130

Mahogany Pembroke table, with one drawer, circa 1830. $505 £225

George III mahogany and tulip banded Pembroke table.
$675 £300

Mahogany Pembroke table on reeded legs, circa 1800
$1,125 £5

19th century burr-walnut and cedarwood Pembroke table, 28½in. wide.
$1,630 £725

Mahogany pedestal Pembroke table, 42 x 46 x 29in., circa 1800.
$1,685 £750

19th century satinwood Pembroke table, 32½in. wide.
$1,690 £750

Early 19th century George faded rosewood Pembroke table, 41¾in. wide.
$1,970 £87

SIDE TABLES

19th century half round mahogany side table on square tapered legs, 2ft. 10in. wide. $225 £100

A 19th century carved rosewood side table. $745 £330

Unusual William IV rosewood side table, circa 1835, 3ft. wide.
$745 £330

19th century French wood side table with ends.
$1,350 £

Regency rosewood pier table in the manner of Thomas Hope, 46½in. wide.
$1,575 £700

19th century boulle side table with ormolu mounts.
$1,690 £750

19th century Dutch floral marquetry walnut side table.
$1,800 £800

Late George III mahogany bow-fronted side table, 2ft.11in. wide, circa 18
$2,250 £1,0

ahogany sofa table, circa
40, 54in. wide.
$500 £225

William IV rosewood sofa
table, 88cm. wide.
$845 £375

Regency mahogany sofa
table, circa 1815, 5ft.
10in. wide. $990 £440

Early 19th century Anglo-
Indian ebony sofa table,
4ft.2in. wide.
$1,125 £500

ency rosewood sofa
e with satinwood
d top, 26in. wide.
$1,125 £500

Regency mahogany pede-
stal sofa table, 59in.
wide open. $1,440 £640

19th century Dutch maho-
gany and satinwood cross-
banded sofa table, 42in.
wide. $1,690 £720

Regency brass inlaid rosewood sofa table, circa
1815, 3ft.7in. wide.
$3,095 £1,375

ncy rosewood and
strung sofa table on
sabre legs on platform
$3,220 £1,430

Dutch marquetry and
mahogany sofa table,
circa 1820, 4ft.2in. wide.
$3,375 £1,500

Regency mahogany sofa
table, 5ft. wide open,
circa 1810. $3,600 £1,600

Early 19th century black
lacquer table, 38in. wide
closed. $5,850 £2,600

all walnut Sutherland
ble with ebonised
rs. $335 £150

19th century solid maho-
gany Sutherland table on
turned legs. $340 £150

Walnut veneered Victorian
Sutherland table.
$565 £250

Sutherland table in maho-
gany with brass inlay.
$785 £350

Victorian games table in
mahogany on a central
column with platform
base. $225 £100

Victorian rosewood work
table with sliding bag.
              $340 £150

Rosewood work table,
circa 1850, 30 x 22½in.
              $430 £190

19th century burr-walnut
work table with diamond
inlay top, 61cm. wide.
              $450 £20

19th century pollard elm
work table with brass
claw castors. $505 £225

Early Victorian sewing
table with drop flaps and a
U-shaped centre support.
              $565 £250

19th century marquetry
work table on fine turned
legs. $675 £300

English walnut and marq-
try lady's work table, cir
1850, 28in. high.$810 £

Mid 19th century ebony
sewing table, 25in. high.
              $845 £375

Late Regency walnut and
rosewood work table in-
laid with brass, copper
and mother-of-pearl, 21in.
wide. $900 £400

Victorian papier mache
octagonal work table inlaid
with mother-of-pearl, 47cm.
wide. $900 £400

Walnut combined work
and games table, 1860
33¼in. wide.$1,010 £

George IV boulle games
table, circa 1830, 1ft.6in.
wide. $1,350 £600

Marquetry walnut work
table with serpentine top,
circa 1870, 20¾in. wide,
interior with removable
tray. $1,665 £740

William IV rosewood games
table with reversible chess/
backgammon board.
              $1,845 £820

19th century Biederm
ebonised and parcel g
globe work table, 96c
high. $4,500 £2

orian mahogany writ-
table on turned legs.
$200 £90

Early 19th century oak
slant top school desk on
brass cup castors.
$550 £245

Maplewood centre or writ-
ing table, circa 1850, 42in.
wide. $565 £250

Victorian oak library table
with leather top, Ameri-
can, 19th century, 38in.
wide. $785 £350

egency rosewood library
ble with plate-glass top,
2cm. wide.
$1,055 £470

William IV rosewood writ-
ing table, 1ft.5in. wide,
circa 1835. $1,170 £520

'Regence' contra partie
boulle writing table, circa
1850, 32½in. wide.
$1,780 £790

Regency mahogany secre-
taire writing table, 43in.
wide. $1,800 £800

19th century red
lle bonheur du jour,
m. high.$2,140 £950

Mid 19th century French
parquetry display cabinet
on writing stand, 153cm.
wide. $2,250 £1,000

George IV mahogany
writing table, circa 1820,
3ft.3in. wide.
$2,475 £1,100

19th century serpentine
front crossbanded bon-
heur du jour, 3ft.3in.
wide. $2,755 £1,225

rge III mahogany tam-
top writing desk with
carrying handles,
. wide. $3,060 £1,360

Mid Victorian walnut and
marquetry writing table,
55in. wide. $3,150 £1,400

George III satinwood bon-
heur du jour on square
tapering legs, 2ft.3in. wide.
$4,500 £2,000

Regency rosewood and cut
brass inlay library table,
151cm. wide.
$9,225 £4,100

TEAPOYS

William IV mahogany teapoy with octagonal hinged top, 14in. wide. $440 £195

Victorian rosewood teapoy on tripod base. $450 £200

A Victorian mahogany teapoy on a carved base. $450 £200

Early 19th century rosewood teapoy on platform base with vase feet. $505 £225

Georgian period teapoy in mahogany, 20in. wide, circa 1825. $790 £350

George III satinwood teapoy on splay feet with brass cup castors. $1,125 £500

Regency mahogany teapoy with ebony inlay, 29½in. high, circa 1810. $1,690 £750

Regency simulated rosewood teapoy, lid inlaid with cut brass scrolling, 15in. wide. $2,025 £900

TRUNKS AND COFFERS ·

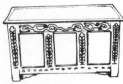

19th century oak hall chest with carved panels to the front, 188cm. wide. $225 £100

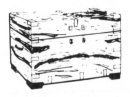

19th century camphorwood trunk with brass straps and corners. $335 £150

George III mahogany silver chest with brass fittings. $620 £27

A Portuguese Colonial teak coffer, circa 1800, 4ft.6in. long, 2ft.1in. deep, 2ft. 3in. high. $675 £300

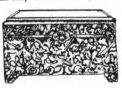

Camphorwood chest, heavily carved in the round, 44in. wide. $720 £320

19th century bombe chest in tu wood veneer with satinwood panels. $900 £400

19th century Dutch burr-elm veneered chest, on bracket feet, 48¾in. $900 £400

Gillow & Co. oak hall coffer, 1870's, 34½in. long. $955 £425

Early 19th century Chinese red lacq leather coffer with brass lock plates 31in. wide. $2,815 £1,250

78

Victorian carved oak hall wardrobe enclosed by two panel doors, 3ft. 5in. wide. $395 £175

19th century mahogany gentleman's wardrobe, 4ft.3in. wide. $450 £200

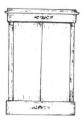

Early 19th century Empire style mahogany wardrobe.$1,010 £450

Early 19th century French cherrywood armoire with brass fittings.$1,900 £845

Rare painted wardrobe, by Wm. Burges, 1870's, 53in. wide. $2,100 £935

19th century breakfront mahogany wardrobe with satinwood banding, 111in. wide. $2,250 £1,000

Ormolu mounted scarlet boulle armoire with arched cornice, 46½in. wide. $2,585 £1,150

19th century Dutch armoire in oak, rosewood and ebony, 6ft. high. $5,175 £2,300

WASHSTANDS

Victorian marble topped washstand on shaped legs. $100 £45

Victorian marble top washstand on a walnut stretcher base. $170 £75

Victorian mahogany wash cistern complete with bowl. $270 £120

Early 19th century inlaid mahogany basin stand with hinged cover.
        $360 £160

9th century rosewood edestal basin stand.
        $420 £185

Early 19th century mahogany corner washstand with undershelf.
        $450 £200

Early 19th century mahogany combined washstand, pot cupboard and commode. $725 £320

George III mahogany campaign washstand/writing desk, 28in. wide.
        $1,465 £650

79

WHATNOTS

Victorian inlaid walnut three-tier corner whatnot with turned supports. $280 £125

19th century ebonised etagere with brass embellishments. $315 £140

Rosewood whatnot, circa 1850, 28in. high. $540 £240

William IV rosewood whatnot with a three-quarter gallery, circa 1835. $810 £360

Victorian walnut whatnot of serpentine form. $810 £360

Victorian walnut rectangular three-tier whatnot, 107cm. wide. $990 £440

Victorian papier mache whatnot. $1,575 £700

Parquetry three-tier whatnot with lobed upper shelf, stamped Holland & Sons and W. Bassett, 21½in. wide. $2,250 £1,000

WINE COOLERS

Large solid rosewood Anglo-Indian wine cooler, circa 1840, 30in. wide. $450 £200

Mid 19th century 'George III' oak wine cooler on stand, 26in. wide. $475 £210

Early 19th century mahogany wine cooler of sarcophagus shape with paw feet. $675 £300

19th century Dutch marquetry wine cooler on cabriole legs with brass carrying handles. $900 £400

Regency mahogany octagonal wine cooler. $1,015 £450

Early 19th century sarcophagus-shaped mahogany wine cooler with original lead lining. $1,035 £460

Georgian mahogany wine cooler, 18in. wide, circa 1820. $1,180 £525

Regency mahogany wine cooler with oval fluted lid, 27½in. wide. $8,100 £3,60

century homeo-
ic medicine chest
twenty-four glass
les, circa 1870, 9in.
$420 £185

Early 19th century mahogany
chemist's chest complete with
fittings. $495 £220

Early 19th century
English apothecary's
chest, 8in. high.
$640 £285

Early 19th century English
apothecary's cabinet, 15in.
high. $1,575 £700

KERS

mian beaker with wais-
ylindrical body, frosted
ll with gilt rim, circa
, 11.5cm. high.
$315 £140

Unusual amber-flashed
beaker of thistle form,
circa 1850, 16.2cm. high.
$395 £175

Lithyalin beaker of cylindrical slightly flared section, circa 1830, 11.4cm.
high. $630 £280

Gilt and 'Transparentemail'
Ranftbecher by Anton
Kothgasser, circa 1820,
11cm. high. $2,700 £1,200

TLES

19th century Zara
liqueur bottle with
postil base.$100 £45

19th century chemist's clear
glass shop sign, circa 1850,
26in. high. $225 £100

Enamelled bottle, circa
1870, 11.8cm. high, with
gilt rim. $325 £145

Serving bottle, dark olive
green with opaque white
inclusions, Shropshire, circa
1800, 12.5cm. high.
$430 £190

LS

cut glass fruit bowl,
liam., circa 1800.
$295 £130

Irish cut glass turnover
bowl, 10in. diam., circa
1800. $460 £205

Palais Royale ormolu
mounted translucent red
bowl and cover, circa 1830,
16cm. high. $900 £400

Very rare double-walled
bowl attributed to Thos.
Hawkes, 4¼in. diam., circa
1830-37. $1,295 £575

CANDLESTICKS

Victorian cut glass candlestick. $45 £20

Silver lustre mercury glass candlestick. $100 £45

19th century Nailsea glass candlestick. $135 £60

Richardson opal glass candlestick, circa 1850. $190 £85

One of a pair of cut glass candlesticks, 9½in. high, circa 1800. $865 £385

CLARET JUGS

Early Victorian ruby glass claret jug, circa 1840. $115 £50

Joseph Rodgers & Sons silver mounted engraved cranberry flashed glass claret jug, Sheffield, 1875, 28.2cm. high. $945 £420

John Foligno claret jug, London, 1806. $1,180 £525

Silver gilt mounted engraved glass claret jug, by R Garrard, London, 1856, 28cm. high. $1,350 £60

CUPS AND MUGS

A glass boot stirrup cup, circa 1800, 6½in. high. $80 £35

Cut glass mug, circa 1820. $115 £50

Small dark brown Nailsea mug, circa 1870, 6cm. high. $155 £70

Early 19th century Swiss gold and enamel zarf, 2½ high. $620 £27

DECANTER BOXES

Mahogany and inlaid decanter box with four cut glass decanters, 8½in. high. $425 £190

Early 19th century mahogany and brass bound decanter case, 22cm. wide. $730 £325

Mid 19th century scarlet boulle tantalus with fitted interior, 13½in. wide. $1,125 £500

Oak decanter box by H. Dobson & Sons, London circa 1850, 9¾in. long. $1,240 £55

19th century barrel-
ed decanter. $90 £40

Large glass decanter, 11in.
high, circa 1830, marked
R. B. Cooper's Patent.
$215 £95

Norwegian decanter of
spherical form, 8¼in. high,
circa 1835. $385 £170

Sunderland Bridge decan-
ter and stopper, circa 1820,
9½in. high. $450 £200

of a pair of English de-
ers, circa 1820, 9¾in.
. $495 £220

Rare Apsley Pellatt encrusted decanters, 10in. high,
circa 1820. $675 £300

Enamelled decanter jug
and stopper with flattened
body, circa 1870, 31.5cm.
high. $790 £350

One of a pair of William
IV mahogany holders and
glass decanters, 1ft.4in. high,
7in. diam. $1,080 £480

RGNES

orian fruit and flower
gne with flared rim.
$125 £55

Victorian vaseline glass vase
with opaque frilly edges on
top and bottom rims, circa
1860, 6in. high. $135 £60

Victorian crimson glass
epergne with centre trum-
pet, 60cm. high overall.
$225 £100

Silver plated epergne, circa
1825, 15½in. high.
$790 £350

ERS

orian cut glass ewer
n fern decoration.
$45 £20

Victorian frosted and cut
glass ewer, 14in. high.
$170 £75

Large cut glass ewer in neo-
classical style, English,
circa 1830, 10½in. high.
$500 £220

William IV frosted glass
ewer with silver gilt mounts
by Paul Storr, London, 1836,
8¾in. high. $7,875 £3,500

FLASKS

19th century Nailsea flask. $135 £60

Bohemian glass flask. $225 £100

Unusual enamelled flask in turquoise glass, circa 1875, 13.8cm. high. $540 £240

German enamelled dated hunting flask, 1802, 5½in. high. $1,125 £50

GOBLETS

Biedermeier green glass goblet, finely etched with deer, 6¼in. high. $180 £80

Good ruby stained goblet and cover, circa 1850, 32cm. high. $395 £175

19th century Bohemian amber overlay glass goblet and cover, 17½in. high. $575 £255

Rare engraved Presentation goblet, 1824, 24.5cm. high. $1,855 £825

JUGS

Victorian cranberry glass jug with ridged decoration, 6½in. high. $80 £35

Mary Gregory glass jug, 8in. high. $115 £50

Nailsea baluster cream jug, clear glass with opaque white decoration, circa 1820, 9cm. high. $270 £120

Unusual glass jug of urn shape, circa 1820, 29cm. high. $745 £33(

LUSTRES

One of a pair of Victorian pink opaque glass lustres, complete with drops. $170 £75

One of a pair of early 19th century Regency cut glass lustres, 9in. high. $370 £165

Mid 19th century overlay lustre, one of a pair, 29.8cm. high. $520 £230

One of a pair of blue overlay lustre vases, circa 1850, 10½in. high. $710 £31?

century Silesian stem-small glass tazza, 3½in. $115 £50

Cranberry glass pipe with white overlay rim to bowl, 16in. long. $100 £45

Victorian cranberry glass bell, 12in. high. $165 £75

Attractive Stourbridge inkwell decorated with millefiori design. $280 £125

and enamelled opaline iture, circa 1835, 14cm. . $450 £200

Bohemian rose water sprinkler, circa 1850, 30.5cm. high. $990 £440

Ormolu mounted amethyst and opaline tazza, circa 1830, 11cm. high. $3,375 £1,500

Biemann portrait plaque of oval form, circa 1830, 8cm. long, probably Franzensbad. $10,800 £4,800

ERWEIGHTS

ber flashed zooglophite erweight engraved with g, 8cm. diam. $340 £150

St. Louis amber flash posy weight, 6.6cm. diam. $495 £220

Clichy patterned mille-fiori paperweight, 8.3cm. diam.$585 £260

St. Louis pom-pom weight, 2in. diam. $865 £385

iature Clichy pansy erweight, 4.6cm. diam. $1,305 £580

St. Louis 'crown' glass paperweight. $2,050 £910

Baccarat double overlay paperweight, turquoise overlay and millefiori centre, 8cm. diam. $3,150 £1,400

St. Louis dahlia paper-weight, 8cm. diam. $9,000 £4,000

RUMMERS

Large engraved rummer, early 19th century, 8¼in. high. $170 £75

Sunderland Bridge rummer, 6½in. high, circa 1820. $290 £130

George III commemorative rummer, 1809, 8in. high. $640 £285

Sunderland Bridge engraved rummer with bucket bowl, 8¾in. high. $745 £33●

SCENT BOTTLES

Mid 19th century painted glass scent bottle. $36 £16

Victorian ruby glass scent bottle with silver top. $45 £20

Mid 19th century Bohemian glass scent bottle. $135 £60

Victorian blue and whit● overlay scent bottle. $115 £5●

Rare sulphide scent bottle of flattened circular form, 7cm. diam.. $370 £165

Blue glass casket with six perfume bottles, circa 1850, 15.2cm. wide. $495 £220

Unusual Baccarat scent bottle, 5½in. high. $790 £350

A gilt enamelled opaline scent bottle and stoppe● circa 1830, 13cm. high. $1,125 £500

TANKARDS

Glass tankard with initials B.H., W.S., circa 1825. $135 £60

Bohemian cut glass souvenir tankard and cover, circa 1840, 25cm. high. $495 £200

Humorous German engraved tankard, 4¾in. high, circa 1810. $605 £270

Unusual hunting overla● tankard, circa 1850, 16.5cm. high. $990 £44●

century engraved fox-ng tumbler, 4in. high.
$250 £110

Early 19th century engraved tumbler, probably by Kugler-Graveur, 10cm. high.
$810 £360

Austrian armorial cut glass cylindrical tumbler, circa 1835, 9cm. high.
$1,125 £500

Bohemian amber flashed hexagonal tumbler, circa 1850, 14cm. high, with engraved sides.
$2,140 £950

SES

of a pair of 19th cen-red coloured Bohemian vases. $295 £130

One of a pair of blue over-lay glass vases, circa 1850, 38.5cm. high. $295 £130

One of a pair of ruby glass portrait overlay vases, circa 1850, 29.9cm. high.
$370 £165

One of a pair of mid 19th century enamelled 'moon-stone' vases, 29.5cm. high.
$450 £200

of a pair of mid 19th ury enamelled vases, cm. high. $475 £210

One of a pair of ruby over-lay vases, circa 1850, 25.2cm. high. $475 £210

19th century Bohemian cut opaline glass vase, 7½in. high.$1,000 £445

One of a pair of English white overlay glass vases, circa 1870, 12½in. high.
$1,045 £465

NE GLASSES

orian ruby wine glass clear glass stem.
$15 £7

U-bowl ale glass with arched decoration, circa 1850.
$25 £10

A Mary Gregory glass de-picting a girl. $55 £25

Hexagonal Biedermeier drinking glass in ruby red with oval gilt banded green panels, 5in. high. $180 £80

87

Rosewood, brass and steel cabinet maker's set square stamped 'A. Surridge', 7¾in. long, circa 1860. $31 £14

Ebony and brass cabinet maker's mortice gauge, 7½in. long, circa 1850. $65 £25

19th century butcher's bone cutting saw with beechwood handle, circa 1860. $76 £34

Beechwood and brass plated brace by Henry Dixon, Sheffield. $130 £60

Optician's sight tester on boxwood measuring arm, 9½in. long, circa 1860. $176 £78

Early 19th century simple microscope with racked column, 4¼in. wide. $225 £100

Early 19th century set of drawing instruments, 5in. long. $250 £110

Manning & Wells terrestrial globe, 20in. diam., circa 1854. $450 £200

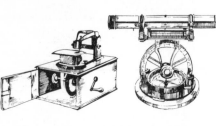

Sewing machine by Wheeler & Wilson, circa 1854. $561 £260

19th century brass theodolite by J. Davis, Cheltenham. $620 £275

Brass pantograph by 'Silberrad, London', circa 1810. $620 £275

Mid 19th century Negretti and Zam... brass binocular mi... scope, 1ft. 2in. hi... $675 £

Set of early 19th century grocer's brass scales by Avery, with ten brass weights. $670 £330

Mid 19th century English zeotype, 14in. high. $845 £375

Mid 19th century Culpeper type monocular microscope, 11in. high. $865 £385

A. Abrahams & Co. brass binocular microscope, ... 6in. high, 1873. $865 £385

88

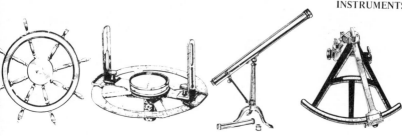

Teak wood and brass banded ship's wheel, 48½in. diam., circa 1870. $870 £385

An English early 19th century surveyor's brass circumferentor. $920 £400

Mid 19th century Wm. Harris brass refracting telescope on stand, tube 2ft. 6in. high. $925 £410

Early 19th century Cary octant with ebony frame, 11½in. radius. $1,045 £465

Early 19th century brass culpeper type microscope, x 441mm. high. $1,125 £500

Good set of mid 19th century Aitken surgical instruments in mahogany case. $1,100 £500

Rare mahogany cased brass gravity sextant, circa 1865. $1,180 £525

Early 19th century Wm. Struthers gregorian reflecting telescope on stand, tube 2ft. 0½in. long. $1,350 £600

Rare James Smith brass monocular microscope, circa 1840, 17in. high, with accessories. $1,420 £630

19th century brass astronomical telescope on a steel stand by Jas. Parker & Son. $1,575 £700

Troughton & Simms refracting telescope on stand, 1857, tube 3ft. 7in. long. $1,855 £825

Rare mid 19th century transit telescope, 16in. high, by Troughton & Simms. $2,025 £900

Superb 19th century hydrometer by Henry Pusham. $2145 £940

Large brass telescope by W.S. Jones, London, circa 1800. $2,250 £1,000

Mid 19th century Johnston 30in. terrestrial globe, 47 x 40in. $3,375 £1,500

19th century portable orrery by W. Jones, 195mm. diameter. $3,600 £1,600

89

Brass cased set of three steel fleams, circa 1820, 3½in. long. $63 £28

One of two early 19th century tin candle moulds, 13½in. $75 £35

A large 19th century polished steel griddle. $90 £40

Heavy cast iron plaque, circa 1850, 12in. high, polished armour bright. $101 £45

Fine cast iron figure of a classical woman, circa 1810, on 5½in. square walnut base. $108 £48

Twisted wrought iron table rushlight and candleholder on pinewood base, circa 1820, 11in. high. $131 £58

Victorian cast iron stove in working order. $135 £60

William IV period cast iron hob grate, circa 1830, 26in. wide. $192 £85

Black-lacquered metal coal bin. $315 £140

Early 19th century painted metal Dutch oven, 27¼in. high. $340 £150

Steel fire grate in George III manner, 84cm. wide. $450 £200

English cast-iron, walnut and marble occasional table with diamond registration mark for June 1845. $475 £210

One of a pair of Victorian cast iron Warwick style jardinieres, 77cm. high. $720 £320

Cast iron 'Gothic' strongbox with hinged lid, 1870's, 13½in. high. $790 £350

Wrought iron gate 1860's 78 x 40in. $1,015 £450

19th century Iranian steel cat with silver and gold harness. $29,250 £13,0

orian ivory sewing
$20 £8

One of a pair of early 19th century candlesticks, whale ivory and baleen overlay on hollywood, 9in.
$110 £50

19th century scrimshaw cow horn, 8in. long, circa 1840, inside curve entitled 'Scotland'.
$130 £58

Hanging scent bottle with painted ivory and seal, circa 1830-40.
$155 £70

d 19th century ivory d for a walking stick.
$225 £100

Large whale's tooth scrimshaw, mid 19th century, 7in. high.
$305 £135

Early 19th century bone watchstand, prisoner-of-war. $370 £165

19th century German ivory crucifix on a wooden cross, 24in. high.
$720 £320

h century Japanese ved ivory figural up, 4½in. high
$765 £340

Carved elephant ivory figure of Guanyin and attendant and Fo dog, 19th century, 12¼in. high. $900 £400

19th century Japanese carved ivory figure.
$1,980 £880

19th century Japanese ivory carving of a travelling salesman carrying baskets, 10¼in. tall.
$2,925 £1,300

century mid Euro-ivory tankard with r mounts, 12½in.
$5,965 £2,650

19th century French carved ivory group, 9in. high. $6,190 £2,750

One of a pair of carved ivory sphinx candlesticks, 11½in. high, early 19th century.
$11,815 £5,250

A pair of ivory figures, circa 1865, French, 29½in. high.
$37,125 £16,500

91

Old Horse coach lamp in black painted tin, wi cut bevelled glass panel circa 1850. $180 £80

Victorian brass desk lamp with white shade. $145 £65

A brass oil lamp on circular base with glass shade. $170 £75

Victorian style hanging oil lamp. $170 £75

Brass hall lantern wit four leaded stained g panels, circa 1860, 22 high. $250 £1

Ship's masthead riding light in copper, 55cm. high. $225 £100

A brass circular oil lamp with crimson glass shade, 23in. high. $225 £100

A tall brass oil lamp with twin reservoirs and frosted globes. $260 £115

Victorian opaline an ormolu lamp for oil, circa 1870, 2ft. 7in. high. $505 £22

A very handsome Victorian oil lamp made in bronze and Paris porcelain, circa 1860. $295 £130

A fine copper pub lamp, with original green glass, 32in. high, circa 1850. $395 £175

Worcester oil lamp on gilt-metal base, circa 1870. $475 £210

One of a very fine pa of Portuguese silver mounted carriage lan 2ft. 6in. high, mid 19 century. $4,500 £2

Regency bronze hanging kolza oil lamp, circa 1820, 2ft. wide. $955 £425

A 19th century gilt brass hall lantern, of octagonal form, decorated with hooves and ram's heads. $1,015 £450

One of a pair of Gothic bronze lamps, 1830, 24in. high. $1,690 £750

plaque of Napoleon
aparte on horseback,
1810, 9½in. high.
$130 £60

Mid-19th century lead
jar with cast and applied
decoration. $135 £60

One of a pair of cast lead
circular plant tubs with
flowers and scrolls in
relief, 13¼in. diam.
$450 £200

One of a set of four mid
19th century lead garden
figures, 25in. high.
$790 £350

9th century lead
of Mercury, 46in.
$900 £400

One of a pair of garden
urns of lead, 2ft. 6in.
high. $1,350 £600

Pair of 19th century lead
figures in period costume,
53in. high.
$2,250 £1,000

19th century lead figure
of Pan, 49in. high.
$4,725 £2,100

le bust of the
e Consort, 69cm.
$225 £100

19th century white
marble statuary bust of
a girl, draped, 68cm.
high. $280 £125

Carved marble bust of
the Duke of Wellington,
28¼in. high.
$315 £140

Mid 19th century marble
bust of a lady by Joseph
Mitchell, 20½in. high.
$505 £225

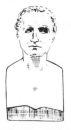

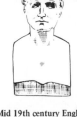

9th century Second
e verde antico
and gilt bronze
n, 39¼in. high.
$900 £400

Mid 19th century English
white marble bust of the
Duke of Wellington, 59cm.
high. $865 £400

19th century Italian
coloured marble bust of
a young woman, 60cm.
$1,610 £700

Mid 19th century Italian
marble figure, 43½in.
high. $4,725 £2,100

93

Early 19th century mahogany framed shield shaped swing mirror. $65 £30

Victorian mahogany framed dressing table mirror with shaped base. $90 £40

Early 19th century mahogany mirror stand, 20in. high. $170 £75

Lady's hand mirror in black lacquer and exc wood case, 15½in. lon circa 1850. $175 £

Victorian cast iron standing or hanging mirror, circa 1850, 14½in. high. $195 £85

19th century brass framed wall mirror, 60cm. high. $220 £95

Early 19th century Italian carved gilt wood and velvet framed mirror. $270 £120

Regency giltwood con vex mirror, circa 1805 2ft. 4in. high.
$495 £27

Walnut cheval mirror, 1850's, 78in. high.
$565 £250

Carved gilt wood mirror, circa 1860, 26in. wide. $885 £400

Large giltwood overmantel mirror, circa 1840, 90 x 70in. $900 £400

Regency parcel gilt ar ebonised pier glass, ci 1805, 5ft. 1in. high.
$1,095 £

Mid 19th century giltwood wall mirror, 50 x 38in. $1,240 £550

Gilt wood wall mirror with carved frame, circa 1860, 41in. wide.
$1,550 £700

19th century pier glass with giltwood frame.
$1,610 £715

19th century Indian c ed teak mirror.
$3,490 £1

A miniature mahogany circular breakfast table, on pillar and block. $90 £40

Miniature 19th century rocking chair. $90 £40

19th century apprentice mahogany chest of drawers, 26cm. high. $135 £60

A miniature mahogany wardrobe, enclosed by two doors, with carved beaded borders, 16in. high, 13in. wide. $135 £60

Miniature Victorian mahogany sideboard with a mirrored back. $160 £70

A miniature apprentice made settle, Brittany, circa 1850, in oak with hinged lid, 12¾in. long. $295 £130

Miniature 19th century piano decorated with marquetry, by W. A. Whittlesey, 14½in. wide. $340 £150

A child's chair made of horns, 18in. high, circa 1820. $475 £210

MODELS

19th century model of an English cottage made from oak. $135 £60

Shell model of 'Broughton Hall', 26 x 13in. $145 £65

19th century model of a gypsy caravan. $215 £95

Victorian model greengrocer's shop, high, circa 1840. $340 £150

Mid 19th century Noah's Ark with 370 wooden animals, 56cm. long overall. $745 £330

French sawmill model in a glass case. $1,070 £475

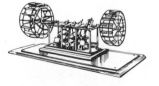

operated working model of enson's 'Rocket' in glass $1,215 £540

Rare mid 19th century model of a twin cylinder reversing oscillating paddle steamer engine, 20½in. wide. $2,165 £980

Early 19th century saddler's model of a dapple grey stallion, 15.2 hands high. $2,700 £1,200

95

MODEL SHIPS

Model English galleon made of wood, with cloth sails, circa 1870. $70 £30

A 19th century scale model of a clinker-built sailing boat, 27in. long. $350 £155

Mid 19th century model of the galleon 'Elizabeth Jonas', 1ft.5in. wide. $700 £310

A model of the Yarmo drifter 'Everest', about 1860-75, signed Charle Saunders. $730 £32

Early 19th century French prisoner-of-war work 'Man-o'-War', 13in. high. $1,015 £450

French prisoner-of-war bone ship model, circa 1800, 8¾in. long. $2,140 £950

French prisoner-of-war model of the frigate 'Venus', circa 1815. $3,150 £1,400

Early 19th century b wood and ebony cop sheathed model of 'L Heros'. $9,450 £4,20

MODEL TRAINS

Rare tinplate French carpet toy train, 15in. long, circa 1870. $235 £105

A Victorian coal-fired model ste engine, 13½in. high. $280 £12

Early spirit-fired brass 'Piddler' engine, mid 19th century, 9in. long.$300 £135

Early tinplate carpet toy train and carriages, French, circa 18 1ft. 7in. long. $620 £27

19th century 4½in. gauge brass and copper live steam coal-fired engine, 1ft.5½in. long. $640 £285

Early live steam locomotive, 3¾in. gauge. $1,375 £610

Model of a North Eastern 18 type Kitson Thompson and Hewitson, Leeds, 2-4-0 locor $2,810 £

al finely carv-ble flute of ood, 13½in. irca 1820. $108 £48

Brass military trumpet, circa 1870, 17in. long. $110 £50

Eight-keyed boxwood clarinet by D'Almaine & Co., London, circa 1850, 23in. long. $305 £135

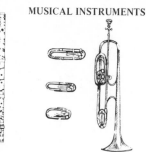

One-keyed boxwood flute with ivory mounts by Cahusac, London, circa 1800, 20¾in. $330 £150

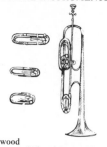

Unusual trumpet by Kohler, London, 24in. long, circa 1865. $360 £160

9th century eide, 41in. $405 £180

UKE

Boxwood four-keyed flute by Rudall & Rose, London, 1840-50, 21in. long. $675 £300

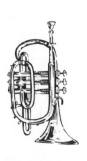

Mahogany cased silver plated cornet, 12½in. long, circa 1860. $675 £300

Boxwood double flageolet by William Bainbridge, London, 19½in. long, circa 1827. $1,125 £500

English Serpent by Thos. Key, London, mid 19th century, 7ft. 8¾in. long. $2,590 £1,150

d ivory netsuke asayuki, early 19th ry, 3.5cm. high. $250 £110

19th century ivory netsuke of the three heroes of Han. $415 £185

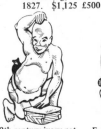

19th century ivory netsuke of a rat catcher, signed Hansaku. $450 £200

Early 19th century ivory netsuke. $530 £235

ned 19th century netsuke. $565 £250

19th century ivory netsuke of Ashinaga and Tenaga. $565 £250

Mid 19th century wood netsuke by Masakazu, 3.5cm. wide. $865 £385

Mid 19th century ivory netsuke, signed Mitsusada. $3,375 £1,500

Very fine pewter cover- ed china jug by E. Ridg- way and Abington Hanley, dated 1855. $85 £35

Early 19th century pewter half pint tankard in the shape of a tulip. $65 £30

Antique pewter belly measure, circa 1820, stamped 'Pint', 5¼in. high. $125 £55

One of a pair of anti pewter beakers, circ 1820, 4in. high. $155 £7

Large 19th century Scottish lidded measure with thumbpiece. $170 £75

Early 19th century one gallon harvest measure with scroll handle, 11½in. high $450 £200

19th century Swedish tapering lidded pewter tankard with ball thumb- piece. $450 £200

A pewter spoon rack b A. Heiddan, Lubeck, ci 1820. $505 £225

French lidded cylindrical measure, 19th century, 11in. high. $565 £250

Scottish pewter tappit hen measure, circa 1800, 11in. high overall. $800 £370

German guild tankard, circa 1800, 29.2cm. high overall. $1,010 £450

Swiss pewter Stegkann with baluster body en- graved with flowers, 1 century, 12½in. high. $1,100 £500

Saxon pretzel baker's guild plate in pewter by Daniel Gottlob Reinhard, circa 1800, 25cm. diam. $1,260 £580

A Scots baluster measure of quart capacity by William Scott of Edinburgh, 20cm. high, circa 1800. $1,350 £600

Pewter Prismen Kann or lidded flask, by F. Cane, Appenzell, Swiss, early 19th century, 36cm. high. $1,350 £600

A rare Irish gallon hay- stack measure by Willi Seymour, 29.5cm. high circa 1825. £1,690 £7

quare piano by Gould-
g, Phipps, D'Almaine
Co., London, circa
804, 5ft. 5½in. long.
$1,070 £475

Early 19th century neo-
classic German walnut
piano by Michael
Rosenberger, 79in. high.
$1,125 £500

Good square piano by
John Broadwood & Sons,
London, in mahogany
case, circa 1820, 173.3cm.
long. $1,800 £820

Grand pianoforte by
John Broadwood & Sons,
London, 1810, 245.6cm.
long. $2,300 £1,050

d 19th century
ennese 'giraffe' piano,
7in. high, in rosewood
se. $2,700 £1,200

Conductor's piano by
John Broadwood & Sons,
London, circa 1815,
92.1cm. long.
$2,735 £1,250

Fine Viennese pianoforte
by Josef Bohm, circa 1810-
15, length of case 88½in.
$3,680 £1,600

Grand pianoforte by
John Broadwood & Sons,
London, circa 1815,
248.3cm. long.
$3,950 £1,800

nd pianoforte by
ph Kirkman, London,
a 1800, 227.3cm.
. $5,900 £2,700

Lyraflugel by F. N. Klein,
Berlin, circa 1840, 6ft. 10in.
high. $6,570 £3,000

Grand pianoforte by
Sebastian Erard, London
and Paris, circa 1840,
94in. long.
$7,425 £3,300

Very rare and important
'Portable Grand Piano-
forte' by John Isaac Haw-
kins, London, circa 1803,
139.1cm. high.
$16,200 £7,400

rian wickerwork
$20 £8

Early 19th century block
Meerschaum pipe with
silver mounts, bowl 9½in.
long. $170 £75

19th century German
pottery pipe, carved,
with copper and
mother-of-pearl stem.
$80 £35

Swedish silver mounted
wood pipe bowl, 5in.
high, maker's mark NW,
1851. $340 £150

RUGS

Mid 19th century
East Persian antique
Belouch rug, 1.87 x
1.09cm. $620 £275

Antique Qashqai rug,
6ft. 11in. x 4ft. 9in.,
circa 1870.
$1,015 £450

Antique Sarouk prayer
rug, circa 1870, 6ft. 4in.
x 4ft. 8in. $2,250 £1,000

Mid 19th century North
West Persian antique silk
Heriz rug, 1.88 x 1.37m
$20,250 £9,000

SAMPLERS

Sampler worked with a
house by Caroline Laver-
stock, 1838, 16 x 11½in.
$90 £45

Sampler by Elizabeth
Brook, 1813, 15 x 11½in.
$145 £70

Sampler worked with a
house and a verse by Maria
Norman, 1832, 16 x 12in.
$265´£130

Child's sampler in good
condition, 1819.
$365 £170

SEALS

Victorian pinchbeck fob
seal. $45 £20

Gold mounted mother-
of-pearl seal, circa 1825,
3¾in. high. $225 £100

Gold musical fob seal,
circa 1835-40,1¾in.
high. $855 £380

A gold musical seal, circa
1820 28mm. high.
$1,350 £600

SIGNS

Etched glass chemist's
sign, circa 1870, 40cm.
wide. $215 £95

19th century double-
sided sheet iron Tavern
sign 'The Prince of Orange'.
$675 £300

Fine raised lead Tavern
sign in wrought iron
frame, 38in. across, circa
1850. $845 £375

A large Royal Coat of
Arms cut in four pieces
painted in true heraldic
colours, circa 1860, 50
x 40in. $2,250 £1,000

Early Victorian shaped circular cake basket with swing handle, 13in. diam., by Hardy, Bell & Co. Ltd., Sheffield, 1839, 34oz.17dwt. $1,070 £475

rian silver plated cake t basket by Philip rry & Sons, Sheffield, 865. $115 £50

Henry Wilkinson & Co. shaped circular cake basket, Sheffield, 1844, 612gm., 22.5cm. high. $520 £230

George IV shaped oval cake basket, 13½in. wide, by Kirkby Waterhouse & Co., Sheffield, 1821, 38oz. 12dwt. $1,295 £575

e III fluted oval cake t by S. Hougham, n, 1803, 14in. long, 3dwt.$1,690 £750

William IV cake basket by E., E., J. & W. Barnard, London, 1830, 12½in. diam., 47oz.16dwt. $2,070 £920

George III oblong cake basket by P. & W. Bateman, London, 1811, 13¾in. wide, 35oz. 13dwt. $2,140 £950

George IV oval cake basket by James Fray, Dublin, 1821, 13¾in. wide. $3,095 £1,375

KERS

am IV silver gilt cy- ical beaker by C. ings and Wm. Sum- , London, 1834, . high, 6oz.19dwt. $945 £420

George III cylindrical beaker, 4¼in. high, London, 1811, 9oz. $1,015 £450

One of a pair of silver gilt beakers by T. E. Seagars, London, 1849, 13cm. high, 875gm. $1,125 £500

George IV silver gilt beaker of Setzbecker form by J. Bridge, 1827, 8oz.19dwt. $1,690 £750

UIT CONTAINERS

George III circular biscuit barrel, 6¾in. high, by S. Hougham, London, 1801, 7oz.14dwt. $1,295 £575

rian oak biscuit barrel lated mounts. $35 £15

Silver plated biscuit barrel or cookie jar, circa 1870, 7¼in. diam. $135 £60

George III silver biscuit box by Benjamin Smith. $890 £395

101

Circular bowl by Joseph Angell, London, 1855, 12.8cm. diam., 258gm. $405 £180

French circular shaped two-handled silver bowl, cover and stand, maker's mark PA/T, circa 1870, 729gm. $630 £280

William IV sweetmeat bowl, London, 1831, 16oz.13dwt., 4½in. high. $990 £440

William IV Scottish bowl by Robert Gra Glasgow, 1832, 10in. 36oz.14dwt. $1,045

An American circular bowl, 5¼in. high, circa 1800, 10oz. 14dwt. $1,080 £480

Maltese covered sugar bowl, by Saverio Cannataci, circa 1820, 6½in. high, 14oz.9dwt. $1,170 £520

George III Scottish circular bowl, by R. Gray & Son, Edinburgh, 1811, 8oz. 8dwt., 5in. diam. $1,350 £600

Large Regency sugar and cover, by Edward Farrell, 1818, 35oz. $1,465

Silver gilt covered sweetmeat bowl by R. & S. Garrard, London, 1839, 24.2cm. high, 2,018gm. $3,600 £1,600

Victorian circular standing bowl by Paul Storr, London, 1838, 76oz.13dwt., 12¾in. diam. $5,850 £2,600

Large circular two-handled rosebowl by Richard Hennell, 1864, 17in. diam., 175oz. $7,425 £3,300

Silver gilt bowl by Ed Farrell, 1820, 17in. w $7,875 £3

BOXES

William IV silver bougie box by Elder & Co., Edinburgh, 1833, 2¾in. high. $295 £130

Victorian vesta box with opening top, circa 1869, 2¼in. high, 3¾oz. $405 £180

Dutch silver tobacco box by H. Kuilenburg, 1849, 5oz.17dwt., 5in. wide. $1,170 £520

South African oval sug box and cover, circa 1800, 8oz.13dwt. $1,855 £8

Sheffield plate five-candelabrum table epiece by James n & Sons, circa , 72cm. high.
$430 £190

A five-light candelabrum, 27in. high, circa 1820.
$540 £240

One of a pair of three-branch filled candelabra in the style of Daniel Marot.
$810 £360

One of a pair of three-light candelabra, 24¾in. high, by M. Boulton & Co., circa 1815.
$1,180 £525

rian silver gilt three-candelabrum centre- , 25in. high, by & Barnard, 151oz.
$4,500 £2,000

William IV candelabrum by E., J. & W. Barnard, London, 1834, 26¾in. high, 174oz.7dwt.
$5,445 £2,420

One of a pair of early 19th century German candelabra, circa 1825, 28½in. high, 225oz.9dwt.
$8,100 £3,600

Regency five-light candelabrum by E. Farrell, London, 1819, 30in. high, 463oz.
$13,050 £5,800

DLESTICKS

e of a pair of H. kinson & Co., a 1840, 9¼in. n.
$405 £180

One of a pair of Victorian table candlesticks, 9in. high, by T. Bradbury & Co., Sheffield, 1845.
$655 £290

One of a pair of Victorian silver candlesticks by H. Wilkinson & Co., Sheffield, 1863, 9in. high.
$675 £300

One of a pair of large Spanish candlesticks, circa 1820, 17in. high.
$890 £395

One of a pair of mid 19th century Portuguese cast silver table candlesticks, maker's mark QAR, 947gm.
$945 £420

of a pair of rge III table lesticks by n Roberts & Sheffield, , 22in. high.
$1,800 £800

One of a pair of George IV table candlesticks, 10in. high, by Robert Garrard, 1827, 51oz.
$2,215 £985

One of a set of four George III table candlesticks by J. Roberts & Co., Sheffield, 1805, 8in. high.
$3,040 £1,350

One of a set of four William IV rococo style silver candlesticks, by J. Watson, Sheffield, 1835.
$3,715 £1,650

One of a set of four Victorian table candlesticks, by Robt. Garrard, 1842, 171oz., 13in. high. $5,065 £2,250

CARD CASES

Early Victorian lady's visiting card case, of mother-of-pearl with silver inlay, 4in. high, circa 1840. $90 £40

Engine-turned card case, by Hilliard & Thomason, Birmingham, 1858. $170 £75

Rectangular shaped card case by Nathaniel Mills & Sons, Birmingham, 1847, 8.7cm. high. $360 £160

Victorian parcel gilt wor visiting card case by Edw Smith, Birmingham, 185 $540 £2

CASTERS

George IV silver pepper, by Thos. Jenkinson, London, 1824. $280 £125

Vase-shaped sugar caster by F. B. Thomas & Co. London, 1900, 22.2cm. high, 568gm. $270 £120

Silver caster, by Samuel Hennell, 1806. $335 £150

One of a pair of George III Scottish casters, 4in. high, by Robert Keay, Perth, 1807, 8oz. $1,295 £575

CENTREPIECES

English electroplated table centrepiece, circa 1861, 56cm. high. $765 £340

Mid Victorian silver plated centrepiece. $1,125 £500

Victorian centrepiece by E. & J. Barnard, 1860, 16in. high, 85oz. $2,475 £1,100

George IV four-light can abrum centrepiece by Ma Boulton, Birmingham, 1 123oz. $5,175 £2,

CHAMBERSTICKS

George III chamberstick by John Moore, 1808, 9½oz. $390 £170

George IV silver chamber candlestick, Sheffield, 1823, 8oz.15dwt. $580 £255

Naturalistic chamber candlestick by Charles Reily and George Storer, 1828, 6½oz. $1,015 £450

William IV silver gilt cha ber candlestick by Paul Storr, 1833, 12oz.3dwt $4,050 £1,8

ffield plate lobed bal-
r coffee jug, sold
sugar basin, circa
0. $260 £115

George IV small coffee pot
by Charles Price, London,
1815, 7in. high, 23oz.16dwt.
                    $900 £400

George III coffee pot on
stand with burner, 11¼in.
high, Sheffield, 1815, 34oz.
18dwt. $1,080 £480

George IV baluster coffee
pot, 11¾in. high, by John
Watson, Sheffield, 1820,
29oz.14dwt. $1,405 £625

Empire coffee pot
ques-Gabriel-Andre
art, Paris, circa 1800,
2dwt., 8¾in. high.
         $1,690 £750

Victorian coffee pot by
W. & J. Barnard, London,
1855, 30¼oz.$1,970 £875

Maltese coffee pot, circa
1820, 10in. high, 31oz.
11dwt. $2,590 £1,150

Early 19th century German
parcel gilt coffee pot and
milk jug by J. G. D. Fournie,
Berlin, circa 1800, 29oz.10dwt.
         $3,825 £1,700

rian frosted glass
th silver mounts,
on, 1842, 5¼in.
         $430 £190

Victorian cut glass claret jug
with silver mount, Sheffield,
1871, 28cm. high.
         $1,015 £450

W. & G. Sissons silver mounted engraved glass claret jug,
Sheffield, 1872, 26.2cm.
high. $1,080 £480

William IV claret jug and
stand by Joseph and John
Angell, London, 1834-5,
36oz.4dwt., 13¼in. high.
         $3,375 £1,500

a pair of George III
asters, 5¼in. diam.,
rge Eadon & Co.,
d, 1803.
         $675 £300

One of a pair of George IV
circular wine coasters, 7in.
diam., by Philip Rundell,
London, 1821.
         $1,295 £575

One of a pair of William IV
wine coasters, 5½in. diam.,
by Edward Farrell, London.
1835. $1,485 £660

One of a pair of Regency
wine coasters by Edward
Farrell, London, 1817.
         $3,040 £1,350

105

CRUETS

Victorian silver egg cruet, 8in. high, by J. C. Edington, London, 1857, 25oz. 2dwt. $405 £180

George III cruet frame, 9¼in. wide, by Abstainando King, London, 1807. $700 £310

George III pierced silver cruet stand, London, 1804, 16oz. $1,125 £500

Table cruet by Paul Stor London, 1811, 30oz. $3,040 £1,3

CUPS

George III Scottish cup, 7½in. high, by John McKay, Edinburgh, 1815, 16oz.13dwt. $385 £170

Hunt & Roskell bell-shaped cup, London, 1856, 16.2cm. high, 490gm. $475 £210

William IV campana-shaped cup and cover by C. Fox, London, 35oz.15dwt., 13¼in. high. $675 £300

Early 19th century silver cup by Paul Storr, 3in. h $1,080 £

George III silver gilt cup, by John Emes, London, 1805, 8½in. high, 29oz. 10dwt. $1,090 £485

George III cup and cover, by Roberts, Cadman & Co., Sheffield, 1805, 56oz. 2dwt., 13¼in. high. $1,240 £550

George III silver gilt vase-shaped two-handled cup and cover, by P. & W. Bateman, 1811, 107oz. $2,815 £1,250

George IV silver gilt stirrup cup by Philip Rundell, London, 1821. $8,550 £3,80

DECANTERS

Victorian silver plated tantalus with three cut glass decanters. $450 £200

English electroplated triform decanter stand, 48cm. high, circa 1860, with three blue glass bottles. $505 £225

One of a pair of silver gilt mounted faceted glass decanters and stoppers, by Reily & Storer, London, 1840, 28cm. high. $2,250 £1,000

George III four-bottl decanter stand by W Allen III, 10½in. hig sold with four wine I $2,700 £1,

...orian silver muffin by J. McKay, Edin-...gh, 1853, 21.5cm. ...1., 19oz. $340 £150

Victorian Irish Britannia silver covered chafing dish, Dublin, 1856, with plated stand and dish, 41oz. $945 £420

Early 19th century Continental silver alms dish, 16¾in. diam. $1,125 £500

French 19th century shaped circular ecuelle with stand and cover by Odiot, Paris, circa 1850, 43oz.13dwt., 10in. diam. $1,395 £620

...iam IV shaped circu-...entree dish and cover, ...in. diam., by B. ...th, London, 1830, ...z.8dwt.$1,520 £675

George III entree dish and cover, London, 1800, 42oz. $1,575 £700

One of a pair of George III silver entree dishes, London, 1809, 98oz. $1,690 £750

One of a pair of Victorian silver vegetable dishes on warming stands. $1,745 £775

...r of dessert stands by E. ...Barnard, London, 1861, ... high, 1,270gm. $1,915 £850

One of two George III oblong entree dishes and covers, 11¼in. wide, by Craddock & Reid, London, 1817-18, 112oz. 13dwt. $2,215 £985

One of a pair of silver fruit stands by John Hunt, London, 1858, 10½in. high. $2,700 £1,200

One of a pair of George III entree dishes and covers by Burwash & Sibley, London, 1807, 123oz., 12½in. wide. $2,815 £1,250

...f a pair of Georgian ...entree dishes, Lon-...823, 98oz. $3,265 £1,450

One of two George III circular sideboard dishes, 17½in. diam., London, 1814-16, 94oz.12dwt.$3,600 £1,600

One of a pair of George III oblong entree dishes and covers by P. and W. Bateman, London, 1810, 133oz. $4,500 £2,000

One of six Georgian second course dishes, 11½in. diam., London, 1827, 155oz.14dwt. $5,850 £2,600

...a set of four George ...l entree dishes and ...by Paul Storr, 12½in. ...41oz.18dwt. $6,190 £2,750

One of a pair of George IV oblong entree dishes and covers by E. Barnard & Sons, London, 1833, 114oz.14dwt. $6,525 £2,900

One of a pair of George III vegetable dishes and covers by Paul Storr, 1807, 113oz., 9in. diam. $7,650 £3,400

One of a pair of William IV oval entree dishes, covers and stands, London, 1833, 239oz. $7,875 £3,500

107

DISHES, MEAT

Shaped oval meat dish with gadroon border, circa 1840, 22in. wide.
$565 £250

George III silver meat dish, London, 1810, 65½oz. $1,240 £550

George III silver presentation dish, 42.5oz. $1,240 £5

George IV shaped oval meat dish by Wm. Eley, London, 1826, 14in. wide, 34oz.11dwt., with cover.
$2,815 £1,250

George IV oval meat dish, domed cover and mazarin, 20in. wide, by Robert Garrard II, London, 1827, 231oz.10dwt.
$4,500 £2,000

One of a pair of George IV s oval meat dishes, by Paul St 1828, 16¼in. long, 100oz.
$8,100 £3,6

EWERS

Italian vase-shaped ewer, 13in. high, by Giovanni Casolla, Naples, 1830, 34oz.18dwt.
$1,405 £625

Chinese silver ewer, 32cm. high, circa 1871, 30oz.16dwt.
$1,485 £660

Martin Hall & Co., vase-shaped silver ewer, London, 1870, 916gm., dented.
$1,845 £820

George IV compress baluster wine ewer b Wm. Eaton, London 1827, 27oz.9dwt., high. $2,365 £

FISH SERVERS

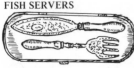  

Pair of Harrison Bros. & Howson fish servers, Sheffield, 1865, in fitted case.
$475 £210

Silver fish slice and fork by Martin Hall & Co., 1872. $305 £135

Cast silver fish slice by W. Trayes, 7oz.14dwt. $1,240

FLAGONS

Victorian silver beer flagon, London, 1855.
$790 £350

Victorian silver flagon, 11in. high, by John Mitchell, Glasgow, 1854, 39oz.16dwt.
$1,575 £700

George IV cylindrical flagon by R. Emes and E. Barnard, 1826, 61oz.
$2,970 £1,320

Large chased and eng silver flagon by Robt. Hennell, London, 185 180gm. $3,265 £1,

Cased silver gilt dessert set by Frederick Elkington, Birmingham, 1876.
$450 £200

George IV 'eagle' caddy spoon, by Joseph Willmore, Birmingham, 1826.
$865 £385

George III picnic set in a leather case.
$1,000 £445

A 19th century canteen of cutlery for twelve persons in a fitted wooden case.
$1,500 £670

t of a Victorian fifty-four e chased dessert cutlery ice by G. Angell, 1859.
$2,025 £900

19th century German table silver by J. F. Brahmfeld, Hamburg, 117oz.
$2,250 £1,000

Two from a set of twenty-four dessert knives and forks by Wm. Chawner, London, 1829-30.
$2,700 £1,200

Part of an eighteen-piece silver gilt dessert service by Martin Hall & Co., Sheffield, 1872, 111oz.
$3,040 £1,350

rt of a George III crested ur glass pattern set of le silver by Wallis & yne, London, 116oz.
dwt. $3,375 £1,500

Part of a set of eighteen German fruit knives and forks, 19th century, with porcelain handles.
$3,600 £1,600

George IV silver gilt dessert service, by Wm. Trayes, London, 1829, 39oz.6dwt.
$3,825 £1,700

One of ten French dessert place settings, circa 1825.
$6,750 £3,000

t of a thirty-six piece sil-gilt dessert service by hols & Plinke, St. Peters-g, 1856. $8,100 £3,600

Part of an one hundred and fifty piece Victorian crested Queen's pattern tableware service by G. Adams, London, 1873, 359oz. $9,000 £4,000

Part of an eighty-four piece George III Coburg pattern table service by Wm. Eley and Wm. Fearn, London, 1823, 172oz.10dwt.
$31,500 £14,000

GOBLETS

Stephen Smith & Son lobed bell-shaped wine goblet, London, 1870, 14.3cm. high, 6.5oz. $90 £40

Bell-shaped silver goblet, London, 1864, 18.7cm. high, 11.5oz. $270 £120

George IV silver goblet with embossed acorn leaf decoration, London, 1823, 12oz. $395 £175

One of a pair of George III wine goblets, London, 181 5½in. high, 16oz.18dwt. $2,205 £980

HONEYPOTS

Silver honeypot by Joseph and John Angell, London, 1836. $1,350 £600

Silver gilt honeypot by A. P. & C. Houle, London, 1860, 11.5cm. high. $1,405 £625

George III 'Skep' honey pot and stand, London, 1798-1800, 12oz.17dwt., 4¾in. high. $1,405 £625

Cut glass honeypot and stand with George III silver gilt mounts by Richard Cooke, London 1800, 5½in. high. $2,475 £1,100

INKSTANDS

Mid 19th century Old Sheffield plate inkstand, 9¾in. long. $260 £115

George Angell silver gilt single well inkstand, London, 1860, 21cm. diam. $495 £220

Small Victorian two-bottle inkstand, by Henry Wilkinson & Co., Sheffield 1846, 12oz.6dwt., 8½in. long. $640 £285

William IV two-bottle inkstand, by Henry Wilkinson & Co., Sheffield, 9in. long, 18oz 5dwt. $790 £350

Victorian silver inkstand, Birmingham, 1851, 19oz., 10½in. long. $955 £425

Silver encrier by E. & J. Barna London, 1852. $1,060 £4

Well modelled Victorian silver inkstand, 8in. wide, 26½oz., 1867. $1,465 £650

George III oblong inkstand by John and Thomas Settle, Sheffield, 1815, 11in. long, 36oz.19dwt. $4,165 £1,850

Early Victorian inkstand, Paul Storr, London, 1837 28oz.16dwt., 11¾in. wide $4,950 £2,2

George IV campana-shaped jug, 9¼in. high, by Wm. Bateman, London, 1823, ?oz.1dwt. $845 £375

George IV small brandy jug on stand with burner, 7¾in. high, by J. Angell, London, 1825, 16oz. 19dwt. $1,240 £550

Silver wine jug by John S. Hunt, London, 1850, 13½in. high. $2,025 £900

French silver gilt vase-shaped jug, 14¾in. high, 31oz., circa 1825. $2,835 £1,260

FFEE JUGS

George IV silver coffee jug, ?in. high, by Richard ?ley I, London, 1827, ?oz.8dwt. $810 £360

George III cylindrical coffee jug, 8¼in. high, by Wm. Burwash, London, 1812, 23oz.18dwt. $865 £385

Chased and bellied Victorian coffee jug by J. McKay, Edinburgh, 1859, 10in. high, 27.7oz. $1,350 £600

George III coffee jug by Paul Storr, 12in. high, London, 1809, 53oz.10dwt. $3,375 £1,500

T WATER JUGS

?hard Sawyer silver balus-?hot water jug with ?ed cover, Dublin, 1845, ?gm. $675 £300

Stephen Smith & Son 'Cellini' pattern hot water jug, London, 1870, 27.5cm. high, 1,362gm. $1,015 £450

William IV hot water jug by J. McKay, Edinburgh, 1834, 9½in. high. $1,755 £780

Silver water jug in the form of a dozing satyr, by Alex. Macrae, London, 1859, 1,380gm. $7,200 £3,200

LK JUGS

?uster milk jug by E. ?. Barnard, London, ?6, 14.5cm. high, 7oz. $145 £65

Fluted baluster milk jug, Exeter, 1850, 15.8cm. high, 251gm. $225 £100

Irish George III silver cream jug, Dublin, 1806. $325 £145

Early 19th century Russian milk jug, 6in. high, circa 1825, 12oz.8dwt. $675 £300

111

Victorian plated dog collar. $405 £180

George III silver bosun's call. $385 £170

19th century Peruvian silver potty, 27½oz. $810 £360

One of a pair of mid 19th century spurs, 8in. lon $460 £2

Large and elaborate Mate pot and stand, 10½in. high, circa 1840, 32oz. 12dwt. $565 £250

Silver mounted Meerschaum pipe bowl, circa 1820, 23cm. wide. $1,240 £550

Cylindrical silver shaving pot with telescopic stand, cover and burner, by R. & S. Garrard & Co., London, 1851, 1,155gm. $1,620 £720

Mid 19th century pierced silver mounted mirror. $1,295 £57

Early 19th century Italian pot pourri vase, 6½in. diam., 31oz.19dwt. $1,575 £700

Large Italian hot water stand and cover, by Pietro Spagna, Rome, circa 1830, 445oz. $13,500 £6,000

Sheffield plate decanter trolley, circa 1810, with ivory handle. $730 £325

One of a pair of stirr with pierced foot res 6in. high, circa 1840 24oz. $385 £17

Mother-of-pearl and gilt metal necessaire as a musical box. $700 £310

Victorian ear-trumpet with ivory earpiece and silver trumpet, by Hawkesworth Eyre & Co., Sheffield, 1845. $1,170 £520

Set of silver sauce labels, circa 1800-25. $710 £315

George Unite silver chatelaine, circa 187 $370 £16

Victorian silver statu- of jockeys by Barnard ., circa 1840, 6¾in. 11oz.11dwt.
$855 £380

Victorian model of a medie- val knight on horseback by J. S. Hunt, circa 1840, 6½in. long. $2,815 £1,250

A fine 19th century silver model of a stag.
$5,400 £2,400

Two silver plated Egyptian cranes, 28in. high.
$5,400 £2,400

GS

r christening mug, 1858. $135 £60

Victorian silver christening mug, London, 1853, 5oz.
$225 £100

Victorian silver gilt mug, 4in. high, by J. Charles Edington, London, 1861, 6oz.19dwt.
$360 £160

Christening mug with child's knife, fork and spoon, by Hunt & Roskell and Francis Higgins, 1867-73.
$1,575 £700

TARDS

ge III silver drum mus- 2¼in. high, by Samuel , London, 1801, 6oz.
$270 £120

Victorian mustard pot by R. Peppin, 1856, 8½oz. $450 £200

George IV baluster mustard pot and spoon by Paul Storr, 1829, 3¼in. high, 6oz. 8dwt. $1,035 £460

Silver gilt mustard pot by John Bridge, 1825, 24oz.
$5,515 £2,450

MEGS   PEPPERS

nutmeg grater by g & Sumners,
$495 £220

Nutmeg grater by W. J., Aberdeen, circa 1830, 1½in. wide. $810 £360

One of a pair of George III vase-shaped peppers by Samuel Whitford II, London, 1809, 5oz. 8dwt. $1,395 £620

Pair of Victorian silver pepper pots, 1872, with glass eyes, 3½in. high, 5oz.8dwt.
$1,800 £800

PLATES

QUAICH

One of six George IV shaped circular dinner plates by Paul Storr, London, 1821, 9¾in. diam., 118oz.9dwt.
$7,425 £3,300

One of a set of eighteen silver plates by Edward and John Barnard, 1859, 8in. diam.
$13,500 £6,000

Hallmarked silver quaich by Hamilton & Inches.
$315 £140

Victorian Scottish quaich by J. McKay, Edinburgh, 1840, 6oz.15dwt.
$900 £400

SALTS

One of a pair of George III gadroon rim salts, London, 1818.
$170 £75

Russian silver salt with original spoon, circa 1874.
$450 £200

One of a pair of George IV salt cellars, 3½in. diam., by John Bridge, London, 1824, 12oz.8dwt.
$465 £205

One of a set of four George III oblong salt cellars, 4in. wide, Sheffield, 1817, 15oz.3dwt. $540 £240

One of a pair of Victorian Scottish salt cellars, 4in. wide, by J. & W. Marshall, Edinburgh, 5oz.8dwt.
$540 £240

One of a pair of George IV salt cellars, 3½in. diam., by Robert Garrard, London, 1826, 17oz.1dwt.
$1,295 £575

One of a pair of George IV salt cellars by Paul Storr, London, 1827, 3¾in. wide, 7oz.15dwt.
$3,715 £1,650

One of a set of four William IV salt cellars by Benjamin Preston, London, 1831, 55oz., 4½in. wide.
$4,725 £2,1

SALVERS

Shaped circular salver by Waterhouse, Hatfield & Co., 21in. diam., circa 1840.
$450 £200

Large English electroplated shaped circular salver, circa 1850, 62cm. diam.
$585 £260

George III rectangular salver by Simon Harris, London, 1813, 13oz. 17dwt., 8in. wide.
$645 £285

Early 19th century American silver salver by John Forbes, New York, circa 1815, 11¾in. wide, 24oz. 14dwt. $870 £38

Victorian shaped circular salver, 16¾in. diam., by Henry Wilkinson & Co., Sheffield, 52oz.11dwt.
$970 £430

George III rectangular salver, 12¾in. wide, by Samuel Hennell, London, 1817, 26oz.18dwt. $1,080 £480

Victorian silver salver, 21in. diam., by Robert Garrard, London, 1856.
$2,815 £1,250

George III salver by Paul Storr, London, circa 1825, 20¾in. diam., 11 18dwt. $6,415 £2,

114

SAUCEBOATS

One of a pair of early 19th century silver sauceboats. $395 £175

One of a pair of George III oval sauceboats by Wm. Sharp, London, 1816, 16oz.2dwt., 7½in. high. $1,350 £600

One of a pair of George IV oval sauceboats by Charles Fox, London, 1823, 9½in. long, 37oz. 1dwt. $2,475 £1,100

One of a pair of William IV shell-shaped sauceboats by Charles Fox, 1836, 34oz. $5,175 £2,300

SAUCEPANS

George IV brandy sauce-pan and cover, 4½in. high, by Emes & Barnard, London, 1823, 11oz.3dwt. $1,015 £450

Large George IV brandy saucepan and cover by James Scott, Dublin, 1824, 5½in. high, 21oz. 10dwt. $1,465 £650

George III tapering cylindrical brandy saucepan by John Brough, London, 1801, 9in. wide, 7oz.16dwt. $1,690 £750

Silver saucepan by James Scott, Dublin 1824. $2,140 £950

SNUFF BOXES

oblong snuff box, probably Chinese, circa 1835, 2¾in. wide. $225 £100

Victorian rectangular snuff box, 3oz.4dwt., Birmingham, 1843. $270 £120

George III oblong snuff box, by John Brough, London, 1814, 2¼in. wide. $430 £190

William IV oblong snuff box by Nat. Mills, Birmingham, 1831, 2½in. wide. $555 £245

orge III rectangular er gilt snuff box by eph Willmore, Birmingham, 1810, 2¾in. wide. $700 £310

George III silver gilt snuff box, 2¾in. wide, by Joseph Ash, London, 1809. $925 £410

William IV oblong snuff box, by Edward Smith, Birmingham, 1830, 3¼in. wide. $1,080 £480

William IV rectangular snuff box, by Rawling & Sumners, London, 1834, 3¼in. wide, 6oz. 11dwt. $1,195 £530

iam IV rectangular f box, by Joseph Willmore, Birmingham, 1836, a. wide. $1,295 £575

William IV silver gilt snuff box, by A. J. Strachan, London, 1830, 4¼in. wide. $1,735 £770

George IV silver gilt oblong snuff box, by Mary Ann and Charles Reily, London, 1828, 6oz.16dwt. $2,025 £900

Early 19th century Swiss musical box, snuff box and watch, 7cm. wide. $13,500 £6,000

115

TANKARDS

Ornate Victorian tankard in silver by Roberts & Briggs, London, 1858, 11oz., 5in. high.
$475 £210

Attractive 19th century Chinese silver 'George III' style tankard. $600 £265

Heavy tankard by Joseph Rondo, Calcutta, circa 1820, 14oz.2dwt.
$790 £350

Regency tankard by Wm. Elliott, 1818, 37oz., 8½in. high. $2,700 £1,200

TEA CADDIES

Sheffield plate caddy with a solid silver plate engraved with a crest set into the front, 1800-10, 4½in. high. $150 £65

Early 19th century Swiss tea caddy, 6in. high, Berne, 12oz.7dwt.
$1,240 £550

George III tea caddy, 4½in. high, 12oz.16dwt., by Wm. Vincent.
$1,890 £840

Square silver tea caddy chased in relief with chinoiserie scenes, by C. T. & G. Fox, London, 1863, 556gm. $2,205 £980

TEA AND COFFEE SETS

William IV three-piece silver tea service, by E., E., J. & W. Barnard, 44oz.
$1,135 £505

William IV Scottish three-piece teaset, by Elder & Co., Edinburgh, 1832, 50oz.
$1,215 £540

George III three-piece teaset, Dub circa 1810, 42oz. $1,440 £64

Victorian three-piece teaset by R. Garrard, London, 1851, 38oz., sold with plated tea kettle on stand.
$1,585 £705

Three-piece Victorian teaset by Marshall & Sons, Edinburgh, 1864. $1,915 £850

George IV three-piece tea service by Emes & Barnard, London, 1826, 49oz.10dwt. $2,250 £1,000

Victorian four-piece tea and coffee service by George Angell, London, 1849, 82oz. $3,150 £1,400

John Edward Terry four-piece silver tea and coffee set, London, 1831, 2,733gm. $4,725 £2,100

Silver teaset by Paul Storr, Londo 1822, 120oz. $24,550 £11,000

Victorian Elkington plate kettle on stand with any handle. $350 £155

Large electroplated tea kettle on lampstand with burner, by Martin Hall & Co., circa 1870, 41.3cm. high. $565 £250

Victorian circular hot water kettle by Hyam Hyams, London, 1858, 50oz.10dwt. $1,125 £500

Marshall & Sons circular tea kettle, Edinburgh, 1840, 25.7cm. high, with later stand. $1,575 £700

liam IV tea kettle on nd by John Fry II, ndon, 1830, 53oz., n. high. $1,745 £775

George IV tea kettle and stand, 15in. high, by Wm. Eaton, London, 1825, 90oz.5dwt. $2,250 £1,000

George III tea kettle on stand, 18in. high, by Wm. Elliott, London, 1817, 105oz.15dwt. $2,815 £1,250

William IV tea kettle and stand by Paul Storr, London, 1813. $5,500 £2,445

APOTS

y Victorian compressed silver teapot Benoi Stephens, 1838, 27oz.7dwt. $520 £230

George III circular teapot by W. & P. Cunningham, Edinburgh, 1802, 14oz.10dwt. $265 £250

William IV circular flat shaped teapot by Smith & Gamble, Dublin, 1832, 35oz.10dwt. $265 £250

rge III oblong teapot by P. & W. man, London, 1812, 21oz.8dwt., a. high. $745 £330

George IV compressed circular teapot, 5¼in. high, by Thos. Wimbush, London, 1828, 31oz.13dwt. $765 £340

William IV teapot, 6in. high, by Benjamin Smith, London, 1832, 33oz. 1dwt. $1,350 £600

cast rococo silver teapot by James ass, Dublin, 1831, 45oz. $1,405 £625

French vase-shaped teapot, Paris, circa 1830, 8in. high, 23oz.12dwt. $2,025 £900

William IV circular melon-shaped teapot, by Paul Storr, London, 1832, 5in. high, 23oz.16dwt. $2,700 £1,200

TOILET REQUISITES

Mahogany toilet compendium with mirrors, trays and bottles. $315 £140

Early Victorian dressing case with nine engraved silver fittings, 1841, 11in. wide. $720 £320

George IV dressing set, silver gilt mounts, by John and Archibald Douglas, London, 1822, 19oz.5dwt. $790 £350

19th century French gilt crested campaign set, 71oz. $2,845 £

TOASTERS

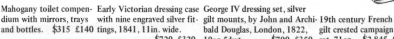

Early Victorian six-section toast rack by Henry Wilkinson & Co., 1839, 8oz. $190 £85

Victorian toast rack by R. Garrard, London, 1869. $280 £125

A silver toast rack by Wm. Eaton, London, 1836, 11oz. $450 £200

Large Elkington, Mason seven-bar toast rack, Birmingham, 1859, 759gm. $1,125 £

TONGS

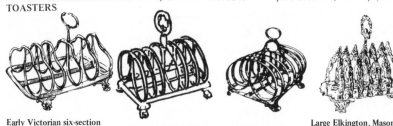

George III scroll engraved sugar tongs, by Peter and William Bateman, London, 1808. $100 £45

Silver asparagus tongs, by G. W. Adams, 1864. $250 £110

Pair of George IV silver grape to by Mary and Charles Reily, Lo 1828, 3oz.7dwt. $350

TRAYS

Antique snuffers and tray in heavy Sheffield plate, circa 1825, 10¾in. long. $80 £35

Victorian silver plated tray with pierced gallery, 25in. long, circa 1845. $620 £275

George III shaped snuffers tray, Wm. Stroud, London, 1806, 11i wide, 11oz.18dwt. $765 £3

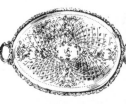

Victorian silver tray, 19in. diameter, London, 1854, 82oz. $2,125 £945

Early 19th century Maltese two-handled tray by Pio Calleja, circa 1800, 10½in. wide, 54oz.10dwt. $2,475 £1,100

Victorian oval tea tray by Atkin Sheffield, 1875, 29¾in. long, 14 19dwt. $3,600 £1

One of a pair of Sheffield plate sauce tureens, part ivory handles and feet, 6¼in. wide. $460 £205

One of a pair of plated oval sauce tureens and covers, circa 1825, 7¾in. wide. $970 £430

Oval soup tureen and cover, 17in. wide overall, circa 1830. $1,240 £550

Oval soup tureen, circa 1830, 16in. long, engraved with armorials below, with gadroon rim. $1,915 £850

Regency two-handled oval sauce tureen and cover by Paul Storr, 1810, 39oz. $2,250 £1,000

French silver circular soup tureen, cover and stand, 5,353gm., circa 1838. $3,265 £1,450

George IV soup tureen and cover, 13¾in. wide, by R. Garrard, London, 1828, 123oz.14dwt. $4,950 £2,200

One of a pair of sauce tureens, covers and stands by Benjamin Smith, 1808, 18.3cm. high, 88oz.10dwt. $16,200 £7,200

RNS

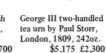

...lian silver plated tea urn, ...¼in. high, circa 1810. $225 £100

Plated 19th century Samovar with domed cover, 19in. high. $370 £165

French silver plated urn, circa 1830, by Balaine, Paris. $585 £260

Oblong tea urn, circa 1810, 17in. high, with shaped square base. $855 £380

...orge III spherical tea urn ...G. Ashworth & Co., ...effield, 1802, 17½in. ...h, 88oz.19dwt. $2,250 £1,000

Large melon-shaped Irish water urn, by T. Smyth, Dublin, 1854. $3,825 £1,700

George III two-handled tea urn by Paul Storr, London, 1809, 242oz. $5,175 £2,300

Presentation tea urn by J. McKay, Edinburgh, 1827, 170oz. $6,300 £2,800

VASES

Early 19th century German oval sugar vase on foot, 7oz. 10dwt. $315 £140

George IV sugar vase by Philip Rundell, 1820, 7¾in. high. $1,125 £500

Large Victorian silver vase by Messrs. Hancock, 1866, 20¾in. high, 203oz. $6,075 £2,700

One of pair of George III silver gilt sugar vases and covers by Paul Storr, 8¼in. high, 61oz.7dwt. $10,125 £4,500

VINAIGRETTES

George III domed octagonal vinaigrette by Samuel Pemberton, Birmingham, 1802, 1½in. wide. $315 £140

Silver vinaigrette in the form of a watch. $325 £145

William IV rectangular vinaigrette by Taylor & Perry, Birmingham, 1836, 1¼in. wide. $370 £165

Silver gilt vinaigrette by S. Pemberton, Birmingham, 1800. $430 £190

George IV silver gilt rectangular vinaigrette, 1½in. wide, by N. Mills, Birmingham, 1828. $450 £200

Silver vinaigrette as a purse by L. & C., Birmingham, 1817. $520 £230

George III purse shaped vinaigrette by John Shaw, Birmingham, 1819, 1¼in. wide. $575 £255

19th century shell-shaped silver vinaigrette. $595 £265

George IV silver gilt vinaigrette, 1¾in. wide, by Thos. Shaw, Birmingham, 1828. $630 £280

Silver book vinaigrette by Taylor & Perry, Birmingham, 1835. $700 £310

Silver vinaigrette in the form of a watch by J. Lilly, Birmingham, 1814. $765 £340

George III silver gilt vinaigrette, 1¾in. wide, by Phipps, Robinson & Phipps, London, 1813. $1,090 £485

George III rectangular vinaigrette, 1¾in. wide, by J. Willmore, Birmingham, 1813. $1,180 £525

George III reeded octagonal vinaigrette by S. Davis, London, 1808, 2in. wide. $1,215 £540

George III vinaigrette by M. Linwood, 1805. $1,890 £835

Silver gilt vinaigrette posy holder with red hardstone ca by T. W. Dee, London, 186 155gm. $2,140 £95

120

mpana shaped wine
ooler, circa 1810,
in. high. $450 £200

Old Sheffield plate wine
cooler with revolving
interior, circa 1800.
$505 £225

One of a pair of George
III Irish wine coolers,
7¾in. high, by James le
Bass, 96oz.5dwt.
$3,375 £1,500

French Empire silver gilt
vase-shaped wine cooler,
10¼in. high, by Jean-
Nicholas Boulanger,
Paris, circa 1800, 60oz.
19dwt. $3,940 £1,750

of a pair of George IV
ana shaped wine
rs by M. Boulton, Bir-
ham, 1829, 184oz.
., 10½in. high.
$6,750 £3,000

E FUNNELS

One of a pair of William
IV wine coolers by R.
Garrard, London, 1835,
120oz. $9,000 £4,000

William IV silver gilt
wine cooler by Paul Storr,
London, 1834, 194oz.
15dwt., 10¼in. high.
$14,625 £6,500

One of a pair of George
III gilt metal wine coolers,
early 19th century, 1ft.
high. $17,550 £7,800

ield plate wine funnel,
1810, with unusual
strengthening sec-
n spout. $135 £60

E LABELS

George III silver wine funnel, London, 1800, 5oz.,
with filter. $350 £155

William IV silver wine funnel by W. Bellchambers,
London, 1833, 7oz., 6in.
high. $450 £200

George III Scottish wine
funnel, 4¾in. high, by R.
Keay, Perth, 3oz.18dwt.
$1,070 £475

rian silver wine label
orge White, Birming-
1867. $55 £25

George IV pierced 'Mad-
eira' wine label, by RC,
London, 1824. $90 £40

George IV silver gilt wine
label by John Reily, Lon-
don, circa 1825.$125 £55

George III pierced 'Madeira'
wine label by P. and W.
Bateman, 1824. $160 £70

e III silver gilt
wine label by W.
nson, 1823, 2½in.
$180 £80

George III cast shell 'Shrub'
wine label by J. W. Story
and Wm. Elliott, circa 1810,
1½in. wide. $295 £130

George IV wine label by
G. McHattie, Edinburgh,
1822. $350 £155

George IV silver gilt
'Whiskey' wine label by
Mary Ann and Charles
Reily, 1826, 3½in. wide.
$565 £250

121

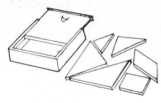

Victorian child's wooden puzzle in box. $12 £5

Victorian child's snakes and ladders game, 16¾in. square. $40 £18

Complete set of wooden skittles, circa 1875. $45 £20

Antique decorated wood 'Pope Joan' game, 10in. diam., circa 1870. $85 £38

Doll's wooden teaset, circa 1870. $85 £38

Victorian child's circular musical box with brass winding handle, 3in. diam. circa 1860. $108 £48

Mid Victorian child's shooting range. $112 £50

A push chair with cast iron frame with leaf suspension, English, 3ft. 7in. long, mid 19th century. $145 £65

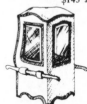

Victorian papier mache pull-along horse, circa 1870. $145 £65

Doll's pram with the original upholstery in black, circa 1860, 24in. high. $160 £70

Set of eleven coloured carpet bowls. $180 £80

An early 19th century model of sedan chair, 11in. high.$190 £

Victorian half tester mahogany doll's bed, circa 1840. $280 £125

A child's galloper tricycle, circa 1870, 3ft.4in. long. $305 £135

A 19th century pair of carved wooden horses. $305 £135

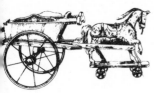

Victorian child's wooden horse and cart. $340 £150

A fine parchment covered toy pony on stand, with pull along wheeled base, circa 1860. $385 £170

Toy stable, German, circa 1860, 2ft. 9in. wide. $395 £175

cale model of a pony trap with original coach painted woodwork in ue and green with yellow lines, rca 1830, 19in. long. $405 £180

Miniature ruby glass tea service with gilt decoration, circa 1860. $475 £210

Old French toy walking clown, 1872, 9in. high. $530 £235

19th century goat and dog cart a child, complete with leather ness, 20in. wide, 68in. overall. $550 £245

Two sections of a glass case containing three scenes from 'Three Little Kittens', 58in. long. $585 £260

A German toy castle made from hand painted pinewood, circa 1850, 19in. high. $620 £275

rian toy theatre showing a sewing in progress. $880 £390

Victorian model of a butcher's shop, circa 1865. $880 £390

Mid 19th century Bavarian Noah's Ark, 19in. long, complete with animals. $900 £400

rly 19th century child's three-eeled carriage. $980 £435

Victorian coromandel wood games compendium in box, 13½in. wide. $1,125 £500

French clockwork tricyclist, circa 1870, with bisque head and original clothes. $1,170 £520

INDEX